"If, as the Bib expressed in the sir songs,' it is surely vital to know how best to that. In *God Sings!*, Douglas Bond provides us with a sure, biblically faithful, and robustly theological guide to thoughtful, God-centered, Christ-exalting, gospel-magnifying praise. In an evangelical world increasingly noted more for triviality than substance, *God Sings!* is a clarion call to the Church to give God the praise of which he alone is worthy."

DR. IAN HAMILTON teaches at Greenville Presbyterian Theological Seminary; and at Westminster PTS, Newcastle, England; and is a Trustee of the Banner of Truth Trust, Edinburgh, Scotland

"In a day marked by the trite and the trivial, Bond calls us back to solid ground. Here is a vision of worship with roots and wings, and the music of a soul enthralled with God, overflowing with song."

REV. NEIL C. STEWART, M.D., Christ Covenant Church, ARP

"*God Sings!* is an engaging book that helps attune our hearts and minds to hear the voice of God in Scripture."

JULIA CAMERON, author, Oxford publicist, and Fellow of the Royal Society of Arts

"Douglas Bond comes to the worship music discussion with the refreshing perspective of a seasoned writer. Instead of platitudes about beauty, glory, and excellence in music, he aims straight at the center —our tendency to idolatry in both pop and traditional realms—while succumbing to the values of a post-Christian culture. It is the only book on this topic that, instead of drawing party lines, invites readers to weigh carefully musical preferences in light of the gospel."

DR. TERRY YOUNT, Chief Musician and Dean, Saint Andrew's Chapel and Conservatory of Music

"Douglas Bond provides a skillful and timely critique of the theological reductionism, musical inferiority, and entertainment-focus of modern worship music, and points us to something far better. I will highly recommend this accessible and instructive book to my own congregation, and to anyone interested in this vital subject."

REV. JON D. PAYNE, Senior Minister, Christ Church Presbyterian, Charleston, SC; Executive Coordinator, Gospel Reformation Network; Trustee, Banner of Truth Trust, Edinburgh, Scotland

"...an inspiringly fresh perspective on the state of congregational singing in contemporary worship—genuine and transparent. Bond's thought-provoking observations are great lessons for anyone passionate about Christ-centered worship. *God Sings!* is a must-read."

MARION READ, professional singer, music educator, and conductor

"Douglas Bond's latest book *God Sings!* is a must read. The wit and warmth of his writing style will engage you, and the plethora of historical anecdotes will delight you. More importantly, the need to recover biblically rooted and theologically rich singing in our churches, families, and lives will challenge you. Buy three copies, one for yourself, and two to give away."

REV. ANDY YOUNG, Minister of Oxford Evangelical Presbyterian Church, UK

"Bond argues compellingly for a recovery of God-honoring, artistically-excellent texts and tunes in the church. An even-handed and witty treatment of a delicate subject, *God Sings!* is a wonderful read—as engaging as it is important. It would be impossible to come away from this book without an appreciation for the best of sacred poetry and praise. So, take up and read—or perhaps better, take up and sing!"

JONATHAN LANDRY CRUSE, pastor, hymn writer, and author of *Hymns of Devotion*, *The Christian's True Identity*, and *What Happens When We Worship*

GOD SINGS!

(And Ways We Think He Ought To)

Also by Douglas Bond

Mr. Pipes and the British Hymn Makers
Mr. Pipes and Psalms and Hymns of the Reformation
Mr. Pipes Comes to America
The Accidental Voyage

Duncan's War
King's Arrow
Rebel's Keep

Guns of Thunder
Guns of the Lion
Guns of Providence

Hostage Lands
Hand of Vengeance
Hammer of the Huguenots
The Battle of Seattle
War in the Wasteland
The Resistance

STAND FAST In the Way of Truth
HOLD FAST In a Broken World

The Betrayal: A Novel on John Calvin
The Thunder: A Novel on John Knox
The Revolt: A Novel in Wycliffe's England
Luther in Love

The Mighty Weakness of John Knox
The Poetic Wonder of Isaac Watts

Augustus Toplady: Debtor to Mercy Alone
Girolamo Savonarola: Heart Aflame

Grace Works! (And Ways We Think It Doesn't)
God's Servant Job

GOD SINGS!

(And Ways We Think He Ought To)

DOUGLAS BOND

SCRIPTORIUM
PRESS

ISBN: 978-1-945062-11-7 (pbk)
ISBN: 978-1-945062-12-4 (ePub)

Cover designed by Robert Treskillard.
Printed in the United States of America

Library of Congress Cataloging-in-Publication Data

Bond, Douglas, 1958-
God Sings! (And Ways We Think He Ought To) /
Douglas Bond. – 1ˢᵗ [edition].
pages cm

ISBN: 978-1-945062-11-7 (pbk.)
1.   Worship (Theology) I. Title.

BT761.3.B66 2014
234--dc23
                                                2013049333

For
Gillian, Giles; Desmond, Shauna, and Otis;
Cedric, Ashley, and Theo;
Rhodric, Tori, Gwenna, Amelia, and Nova;
Brittany, Jesse, and Margot

"The LORD your God is in your midst,
a mighty one who will save;
he will rejoice over you with gladness;
he will quiet you by his love;
he will exult over you with loud singing."
  Zephaniah 3:17

"How greatly did I weep in thy hymns and canticles, deeply moved by the voices of thy Church so sweetly singing."
  Augustine

"I play the notes as they are written, but it is God who makes the music."
  J. S. Bach

"We must beware lest our ears be more intent on the music than our minds on the spiritual meaning of the words."
  John Calvin

CONTENTS

INTRODUCTION

Passionate as I am about singing "psalms, hymns, and spiritual songs," I began writing about singing in worship back in the last millennium in my Mr. Pipes books, a four-volume series of adventure books for children set in the places where hymn writers lived, ministered, sang, and died. Somehow those books have managed to go into multiple reprints and remain in print more than twenty years later, for which I am deeply grateful.

Along the way, I have been asked to write biographies of hymn writers (for Ligonier's Reformation Trust, and Evangelical Press), and to speak at churches and conferences, and Church history tours about what and how we sing in our corporate worship. Much to my astonishment, I was even asked to consult for the Canadian Broadcasting Corporation on their God's Greatest Hits television series. Meanwhile, with fear and trepidation, I began trying my hand at writing New Reformation Hymns (see Appendix).

My goal in *God Sings (And Ways We Think He Ought To)* is to compare and contrast how God and his people sing in the Bible, and in two millennia of Church history, with how we are attempting to do so in recent decades, with the best of intentions, in an entertainment ethos.

It would be impossible to overstate the role of singing in the Bible. Everywhere you turn people are doing it. The book of the Bible with more pages, verses, and chapters than any other is a book of songs, the Psalms, right in the very middle of the Bible. During his earthly ministry Jesus often quoted psalms, and while dying on the cross, some of his final words were from those inspired lyrics.

Singing must be of great importance to God, whom Zephaniah tells us "exult[s] over [us] with loud singing" (3:17). God himself sings. If singing is so important to God, it must be of essential importance to every Christian. The purpose of this book is to explore how God sings, and how he must want his people to sing back to him in corporate worship.

My ultimate purpose is grounded in what Paul wrote: "Let the word of Christ dwell in you richly as you teach and admonish one another with all wisdom, and as you sing psalms, hymns and spiritual songs with gratitude in your hearts to God. And whatever you do, whether in word or deed, do it all in the name of the Lord Jesus, giving thanks to God the Father through him" (Colossians 3:16-17).

1

HOW DOES GOD SING

"The LORD your God is in your midst,
a mighty one who will save;
he will rejoice over you with gladness;
he will quiet you by his love;
he will exult over you with loud singing."
Zephaniah 3:17

God sings! What a remarkable phenomenon to consider. What must God's singing sound like? Finite human voices are limited in range to soprano, alto, tenor, and bass; but what must God's infinite voice sound like? The richest, deepest, most resonate bass voice; the most transcendent soprano, never shrill, never harsh, never shattering, but power and sweetness emanating out of divine perfection. The mere speculation boggles the imagination.

So it is with all genre of the arts. God is the supreme creator, and as his creatures, we do in miniature what he has done and continues to do in infinite grandeur: paint,

13

sculpt, design grand cathedrals, write poetry, and create music. "It is the artist," wrote Solzhenitsyn, "who realizes that there is a supreme force above him and works gladly away as a small apprentice under God's heaven."

Atheist artists can and do create art that, contrary to their own intentions, brings glory to God. But Solzhenitsyn is underscoring the authenticity of true artists who are intentional about their subordinate role beneath *the* True Artist, doing all that they do with their art to the glory of Creator God.

In his book *The Great Divorce*, C. S. Lewis comes at a similar observation but from the negative. "Every poet and musician and artist, but for Grace, is drawn away from the love of the thing he tells, to the love of the telling." That is to say, artists are easily drawn into self-adulation; the love of their craft easily morphs into the love of themselves as they write, or paint, or create music; self-love, thus, usurping the love and glory of God.

Artists who forget the true order of things in the universe, begin to have delusional thoughts of themselves and their creations. Things become inordinate, everything switched around as they attempt to shuffle aside the Creator and replace him with themselves.

It is our most fundamental problem. We do it every day, but how much more so in the arts where human beings are in that god-like role of creating. So enthralled can we become with performance art, we are tempted to lavish upon subordinate creators what belongs only to Creator God himself. We prefer the eyes and ears of sight rather than those of faith. Hence, the ubiquitous idol worship of celebrity singers and performers we can see and hear on the stage. This is no new thing. When Sophocles died, the greatest dramatist of the Golden Age in Greece, the senate made him a god to whom pagan worshipers were to give homage.

How easily we slip into thinking of human beings as ultimate originals rather than creatures. We even borrow divine names and give them to the best artists.

DIVA

"Divine One," the New York Times dubbed Sarah Vaughan, perhaps the finest jazz vocalist of all time. Her effortless three-octave-ranged voice earned her the title Diva, a derivation of the word for a female deity or goddess. Divo, the masculine version of the title, is reserved for the most god-like male tenors. Unwittingly, even the music world assumes that God's voice is the measure of the finest human voice.

If God our creator sings, nothing makes more sense than that we must sing. It makes sense to us that the psalmists sang (Psalm 13:6), that Moses and Miriam sang (Exodus 15), even that morning stars sang (Job 38:4); that pastures, meadows, hills, and valleys shout for joy and sing (Psalm 65:13). It makes sense to us that the angel heralds proclaimed Christ's birth to the shepherds in song (though Luke actually recorded that the angels *said* "Glory to God in the highest").

The gospel accounts of Jesus and his disciples singing a hymn together in the upper room at the Last Supper (Matthew 26:30; Mark 14:26) begin to awaken our imagination about God singing. Imagine listening in at the keyhole to the voice of Jesus singing a hymn with his disciples. What did that sound like?

I imagine the prophet Zephaniah (3:17) was embodying the entire work and ministry of our Savior when he wrote: "The LORD your God is in your midst, a mighty one who will save; he will rejoice over you with gladness; he will quiet you by his love; he will exult over you with loud singing."

Herein is the gospel: God with us, in our midst, mighty to save us, rejoicing with gladness over his bride, quieting us with his love, and exulting—elated, triumphant, bursting with joy—over his people in loud singing.

It seems topsy-turvy. Ruined sinners, such as we, rescued, snatched from the burning, we have infinite reasons to exult in the saving mercy of our loving God in song, but here we learn that this thrice-holy God exults over *us* with singing—with *loud* singing.

REVERENCE AND AWE

If God sings over his church, his church will want to know what that singing is like. If God rejoices over his church, if he quiets us with his love, if he exults over us with loud singing, then we will want to offer back to him sung worship most in keeping with his singing, with his voice.

Christians of all people ought supremely to care about music, about singing. Next to the preaching of the Word of God, singing, seen throughout the pages of God's Word, is central to Christian worship. God speaks to us in the Word, as Luther had it, and we respond to his voice with our own voices in singing.

Does the Word of God guide us in how we are to sing in worship? One could argue that the entire book of Psalms gives us the most comprehensive model of how we are to enter into the presence of God in our sung worship. But if we are looking for a single text, the author of Hebrews gives us one of the most succinct summations of how and why we enter the presence of God in worship. "Therefore let us be grateful for receiving a kingdom that cannot be shaken, and thus let us offer to God acceptable worship, with reverence and awe, for our God is a consuming fire" (12:28-29).

The author of Hebrews lays down several things in an imminently clear and logical order in this passage. Firstly, he believes that there is acceptable worship and unacceptable worship. He then proceeds to tell us without equivocation what the characteristics of acceptable worship are: Reverence and awe. Why reverence and awe? The author goes on to remind us of something of first importance about God's character. The God into whose presence we enter in worship, the God who exults over us with loud singing, and calls us into his presence to sing like he sings—is a consuming fire. There is caution and sobriety in this description. From this text, we are forced to conclude that the worship of God is no place to come half-cocked, with a reckless, casual, cool, or hip manner. On the contrary, everything about our worship ought to be marked by reverence and awe, including the exultant joy and gratitude expressed in our singing.

IMMINENCE AND TRANSCENDENCE

Many in the church today might hasten to object. All this about worshiping with reverence and awe makes it sound like God is distant, detached, far off, a transcendent deity. We're not Deists. We believe in God's imminence; we want to worship a God who has come to dwell among us, a God who is right here, incarnate, Emmanuel, God with us. All that about transcendence and reverence and awe, isn't that the God of the old covenant? Jesus is our brother and he's one of us, right here in our midst.

It's no coincidence that me-centered egalitarianism has produced a decided preference for God's imminence over his transcendence. The contemporary church is far more comfortable with God being born in a manger in humble Bethlehem than it is with God as a consuming fire, who is to be worshiped "in the splendor of holiness," who "sits enthroned as king forever" (Psalm 29).

We're no more at liberty to construct a God who fits within our tidy little box than we are at liberty to enter his presence in worship with casual overfamiliarity rather than reverence and awe. "He is not a tame lion," as C. S. Lewis put it. We can be certain that we are offering un-acceptable worship if we are not worshiping both the God who is in our midst and who is at the same time to be approached with reverence and awe because he is "a consuming fire."

18

IMITATING GOD'S SINGING

If this God who is a consuming fire is also in our midst when we gather as a church to worship him, as Zephaniah tells us he is, we will want to scour the Scriptures to find out how he sings, and how we can imitate his voice.

Surely, imitate isn't the right word. To our modern ears, imitating sounds so rote, like we're just aping God, going through motions. We place such a premium on spontaneity, on personal expression, on taste, on doing things our way. But imitate is an intensely biblical word. We're told twenty-eight times in the New Testament to imitate Jesus Christ and others who are imitating him. "Therefore, be imitators of God, as beloved children. And walk in love, as Christ loved us and gave himself up for us, a fragrant offering and sacrifice to God" (Ephesians 5:1-2).

We are told to have the mind of Christ, to love as he loved us first, to serve as he served us, to give as he gave of himself for us, on our behalf, securing our everlasting bliss by his woe. And in the 122 times that the Bible commands us to sing (and legions more that imply singing) we will want to ask: How does God sing? What does God's voice, the God who is in our midst and who is a consuming fire, whom we are to approach in worship with reverence and awe, what does his voice sound like?

There may be no other single passage of Scripture that more specifically tells us what God's voice sounds like than Psalm 29:

19

Ascribe to the LORD, O heavenly beings,
  ascribe to the LORD glory and strength.
2 Ascribe to the LORD the glory due his name;
  worship the LORD in the splendor of holiness.
  3 The voice of the LORD is over the waters;
  the God of glory thunders,
  the LORD, over many waters.
4 The voice of the LORD is powerful;
  the voice of the LORD is full of majesty.
  5 The voice of the LORD breaks the cedars;
  the LORD breaks the cedars of Lebanon.
6 He makes Lebanon to skip like a calf,
  and Sirion like a young wild ox.
  7 The voice of the LORD flashes forth flames of fire.
8 The voice of the LORD shakes the wilderness;
  the LORD shakes the wilderness of Kadesh.
  9 The voice of the LORD makes the deer give birth
  and strips the forests bare,
  and in his temple all cry, "Glory!"
  10 The LORD sits enthroned over the flood;
  the LORD sits enthroned as king forever.
11 May the LORD give strength to his people!
  May the LORD bless his people with peace!

Let's be clear, as with all of God's attributes, some
are communicable and others are not. We should not
strive to sing in worship in such a way that our voices
break cedars and flash forth flames of fire. But our voice
ought to reflect the majesty and power of God's voice;
we will want to strive for singing that invokes the awe
and wonder wherein all who hear cry "Glory!" We will
want to sing in such a way that the "splendor of

holiness" is felt and known by all who sing. We will want to sing in a fashion that ascribes glory to him, the glory that is due to his name alone, that is fitting and appropriate to these high objectives.

THE VOICE OF GOD

We should not expect unbelievers to think much of God's voice. The serpent in the garden didn't either; the first words he spoke were to disparage and cast doubt on the voice of God: "Did God actually say" (Genesis 3:1)?

Perhaps this is why C. S. Lewis has Uncle Andrew repulsed when hearing Aslan's voice in *The Magician's Nephew*, "He had disliked the song very much. It had made him think and feel things he did not want to think and feel." Unbelievers should not be expected to like how God or his people sing. Fools who say there is no God should not be consulted on the merits of God's singing or of ours. Neither ought we to fashion singing or any dimension of Christian worship after the appetites of unbelievers. Imagine David consulting the Philistines as he crafted the hymnal of the old covenant. Nothing could be more wrongheaded.

But when the Spirit of God begins his gracious work, convicting us of sin and drawing us to the Savior, something changes. Our ears are tuned differently. What used to repulse now beckons us, draws us in. Augustine tells us he was wooed to Christ in significant part by "the church so sweetly singing."

I wonder if C. S. Lewis was musing on Psalm 29 and Zephaniah 3:17 about God singing when he wrote the creation of Narnia scene:

21

A voice had begun to sing... it seemed to come from all directions at once... Its lower notes were deep enough to be the voice of the earth herself. ...it was beyond comparison, the most beautiful noise he had ever heard. It was so beautiful Digory could hardly bear it... Then two wonders happened at the same moment. One was that the voice was suddenly joined by more voices than you could possibly count.

Difficult as it is to describe one medium of art using another, Lewis here employs words that awaken our listening, words that draw us in and make us hear the voice of Aslan singing the world into being, singing "so beautiful Digory could hardly bear it." As we read the words, we feel wonder so deep, thrill so beautiful, reverence and awe so majestic we, like Digory, can barely support it.

As the light began spreading over the creation scene, Lewis records, "All the time the Voice went on singing... now louder, more triumphant.... The Voice rose and rose, till all the air was shaking with it... it swelled to the mightiest and most glorious sound..."

Maybe we need to be more like Lewis's noble London cabby, "'old your noise, everyone. I want to listen to the moosic." When God sings, surely it must be the mightiest and most glorious sound, and we will not want any noise—even and especially the bombast of instrumental noises—to compete with his voice.

Should we expect the unbelieving world to appreciate what and how we sing? How did Satan respond to God's voice? He immediately schemed to contradict it. How did Uncle Andrew and the Witch respond to the glorious voice of Aslan singing the world into being? They "hated it." Our current contortions to get the world to like how we sing, notwithstanding, this should not entirely surprise us.

How, then, do we join in the song? How do we sing as God sings? Surely, it must begin with a transformation of our hearts that results in a right response to God's voice. "The Christian gets his songs from God," wrote C. H. Spurgeon. "God gives him inspiration, and teaches him how to sing: 'God my Maker, who gives songs in the night'" (Job 35:10).

Like Elihu whose "heart yearned within" him at the glorious mystery of God's sovereign ways, so our hearts must yearn, not for what's cool, not for the latest thing, but for the unchanging splendor of God himself. Then we will be able to respond with reverence and awe, all that is within us overwhelmed like Lewis's Pevensie children at Aslan's singing: "Every drop of blood tingled in the children's bodies."

2

WHY WE WAR ABOUT MUSIC

I love going to live performances of Handel's *Messiah* in the Christmas season. While in Dublin, Ireland, we visited the site where it was first performed April 13, 1742. I wanted to break out into the "Halleluiah Chorus" or "Worthy is the Lamb," but my wife managed to restrain me.

Singing in several choirs in high school and college, I'm just enough of a singer to be dangerous. My problem when listening to choirs is that I desperately want to join in, hum the bass line, my wife elbowing me in the ribs and scowling, probably because of the quality of my humming.

I have several friends who are accomplished musicians, organists, vocalists, cellists (my favorite instrument), and I stand in awe of their skill. Though I can hear the difference between my voice and a professional baritone (there is a vast difference), nevertheless, I love to sing. I feel the urge to sing. I was made to sing, made to worship, made in God's image to worship my Maker. "We sing," wrote Keith Getty, "because we're created to, commanded to, and compelled to." If God created us to sing, and he made us in his image, nothing makes more sense—of course God sings!

How sad it is, then, that the thing we are created, commanded, and compelled to do together we end up fighting and quarreling about. Why do we do that, war about worship? As near as I can tell, it's because worship is the most important thing we humans do now, and the thing we will be engaged in for all eternity, singing to and with God himself. Because singing ought to be one of the most participatory dimensions of Christian worship, we tend to have intensely strong opinions about it.

LUTHER'S STRONG OPINIONS

Martin Luther did too: "I have no pleasure in any man who despises music. It is no invention of ours: it is a gift of God. I place it next to theology. Satan hates music: he knows how it drives the evil spirit out of us." Luther extolled the "perfect wisdom of God in his wonderful work of music," and in irascible Luther style, he denounced "He who does not find [music] an inexpressible miracle of the Lord is truly a clod and is not worthy to be considered a man."

An avid appreciator of music, C. S. Lewis after his conversion in 1931 quickly developed strong opinions about congregational singing, strong and rather low opinions: "I naturally loathe nearly all hymns; the face and life of the charwoman in the next pew who sings them, teach me that good taste in poetry or music are not necessary to salvation."

Even agnostic Ralph Vaughan Williams in his Preface to *The English Hymnal* wrote, "Good music for worship is a moral issue. The eternal gospel cannot be commended with disposable, fashionable music styles, otherwise there is the implication that the gospel itself is somehow disposable and temporary."

Williams was writing in 1906, but keep going further back in history and you will find the same thing, even among pagans. Everybody knows the power that resides in music, power for good and for ill—everybody.

"This new music," wrote one critic, "is promoting the moral degeneracy of our adolescents." You're thinking that a fundamentalist evangelist said this, or maybe Mr. Pipes, right? Wrong. It's a quotation from Plato, writing in the Golden Age of Greece in the 5th century BC.

Even the Devil has strong opinions about worship and music (if Lewis's Screwtape can be trusted). In *Screwtape Letters*, C. S. Lewis described heaven as a region of music and silence. The demon Screwtape is frustrated by this reality: "Music and silence—how I detest them both!" He boasts that in hell, "The melodies and silence of Heaven will be shouted down in the end. But I admit we are not yet loud enough, or anything like it."

Alas, some contemporary church growth enthusiasts seem to agree. "We are loud," chortled one California pastor. "We are really, really loud. I say, 'We're not gonna turn it down.'"

I've been in contemporary services where the music was so loud, I could not hear anyone on either side of me singing, nor could I hear myself. The error, well-intentioned though it may be, is in making the instruments loud, not the voice of the congregation. In this kind of setting, however loudly we sing, it doesn't matter; the technological instrumentation has drowned out the voice of the worshipers.

But there will be volume and force behind passionately sung worship. Not emotive breathy crooning, but loud shouts of gratitude and praise. There will be vigor and volume in heart-felt sung worship.

"Sing aloud..." we are commanded in Psalm 81:1-3: "Raise a song..." "Blow the trumpet..." "Shout for joy..." And in Psalm 33:3, we're called to "Sing to him a new song; play skillfully on the strings, with loud shouts."

Whichever side of the war you are on, neither side can argue biblically against loud music. But, biblically, it is always the human voice that is loud, supported by instruments played skillfully, though never so loudly that they drown out the voice of the worshipers. Even loud trumpets and cymbals appearing not infrequently in the psalms will not drown out the voices of thousands of Israelites raising a song and shouting for joy before the Lord. Though, with the flick of a lever, electronically amplified volume can completely subsume the voices of an entire mega-church congregation.

MUSIC AS THE MEANS OF GROWTH

Though the Bible includes no clear musical notation, for centuries Christians arranged their churches and selected their music by searching the Scriptures to answer some form of the question, "What music does God like to listen to?" That has largely changed.

Contemporary worship advocates generally ask: "What does the culture in our demographic like to listen to?" Hence, in recent decades loud entertainment music became the unchallenged strategy for building numbers in the mega church. Regulating their music choices by what the world likes to listen to, these advocates made church growth into the all-excusing rationale for the entertainment ethos, concluding with the credo that pop entertainment music is essential to church growth. They assure us that it's working. "Right after we made that decision [to be a loud, contemporary-music-only church] and stopped trying to please everybody," claimed one growth guru, his church "exploded with growth."

Music once conceived as a means of grace, according to the new theory, has now become music as the means of growth.

But is it truly working? A 2019 Pew Research Center study found otherwise. In a single decade, the number of Americans who identify as "Christian" plummeted by more than 12%. The number of young millennials, the target audience of entertainment worship, declined in the same decade by more than 16%. If churches are supposed to be exploding with growth in this same decade, why the sharp decline in self-professed Christians? Maybe it's not working after all. Maybe it's not working because it can't work. It's not God's way.

UNUSUAL CREDO

The late Neil Postman, in his book *Amusing Ourselves to Death* cites the executive director of the National Religious Broadcasters Associations who seems to agree with the church-growth philosophy: "You can get your share of the audience only by offering people something they want."

Postman, though no Christian, made the perceptive observation: "This is an unusual religious credo. There is no great religious leader—from the Buddha to Moses to Jesus to Mohammed to Luther—who offered people what they want. Only what they need."

When the Church fashions worship to bring unchurched people in by entertaining them, to give people what they want, it inevitably creates, as one journalist termed it, "a Christian ghetto watering down the gospel."

Why do we get so worked up about all this? Isn't it just okay for everybody to do it their way, the way that comes easiest to them? Why do we insist on being right, and look down our noses at everybody else who does it wrong? Luther considered music "the handmaiden of theology." But we insist that it be our music not theirs that is the handmaiden.

It's not just we traditionalists who do this, though we do it with a high brow and believe we have the intellectual, aesthetic, and theological high ground, and Church history to support us. On the other hand, the culturally relevant church looks at those who sing hymns, or at least who sing them in a traditional way, and has decided that they are not missional, that because traditionalists do music without drums and electric guitars, they must not care about the lost.

CHOOSING CHURCH FOR THE MUSIC

Now let's be honest here (honesty being an important step to making peace). It's not just "them." We traditionalists have our version of doing this as well. We all do this, each in our own way.

In an essay on church music in his *Christian Reflections*, Lewis observed: "The first and most solid conclusion which (for me) emerges is that both musical parties, the High Brows and the Low, assume far too easily the spiritual value of the music they want."

Which pill do I need to take? Some can be so busy taking the speck out of the eye of the church and its leaders who use the entertainment model for worship that we become oblivious to the log jutting out of our own eye, out of my eye. This, too, works both ways.

Sinclair Ferguson referred to the danger of using "music for its own sake," in worship. He draws a line between "...going to a service 'for the worship' and going to a service 'to worship the Lord.' The distinction appears to be a minor one, but it may imply the difference between the worship of God and the worship of music!" This, too, works both ways.

Both sides nod in agreement, both the high brows and the low. I know people who go to a church because it has such lovely music, and I know others who go to a church because it has such loud and cool, hipster music. We can make idols out of anything, ironically, even out of the kind of worship music we want, the kind that has the power to move us.

"We know by experience," wrote John Calvin, "that music has a secret and almost incredible power to move hearts." It's precisely because of that incredible power that we get so worked up about the spiritual value of the music we prefer. Calvin knew, however, that powerful things can be both friend and foe. "We must beware lest our ears be more intent on the music than our minds on the spiritual meaning of the words. Songs composed merely to tickle and delight the ear are unbecoming to the majesty of the Church and cannot but be most displeasing to God."

A millennium before Calvin, Augustine wrote approvingly of church singing, but added strong caution. "Nevertheless, when it happens that I am more moved by the song than the thing which is sung, I confess that I sin in a manner deserving punishment."

By which are we being moved, the song (and the performance style of the music) or by the objective content of the lyric we are singing?

WHERE BLESSING RESTS

If it is a war, the entertainment model believes that the war is decisively over and that they long ago came out on top. Measured in sheer numbers of congregations conforming to the entertainment ethos, they are right. On the other hand, I wonder if some of us want a cease fire as much as we may think we do.

Perhaps the only way to achieve a cease fire in the worship wars is to own up to the fact, obvious to everyone else who cares to look at all closely, that our engagement in the debate is more often motivated by pride than clarity of argument, lovingly engaged. We think we are right and the other side is wrong, and that it really matters to be right like we are and not wrong like they are. And it is very important to make sure that we denigrate the cultural refinement or the cultural savvy of the other guys. Most of us, on either side, find plenty to denigrate.

C. S. Lewis's observation about church music offers a possible way forward for those on either side of the front line of the worship war: "There are two musical situations on which I think we can be confident that a blessing rests." He proceeds to show us a leader with refined and cultured musical tastes and training, but who, to a degree, sets aside his preference out of love for those who have coarser musical preferences. Conversely, he shows us a man with those coarser musical preferences who, also out of love for others, attempts to cultivate an appreciation of music he little understands or likes. Lewis then flips the scenarios around and shows us the unblessed spirit of those with only contempt and animosity for the musical preferences of the other side.

Though both sides might hasten to point out Lewis's altruism, he rightly guides both of us in the direction of love and deference to our neighbor.

LOOK AT ME

Late rock musician Keith Green, one of the vanguards of the contemporary Christian music movement himself, honestly admitted some of the problem: "It isn't the beat that offends me, nor the volume—it's the spirit. It's the 'look at me!' attitude I have seen at concert after concert, and the 'Can't you see we are as good as the world!' syndrome I have heard on record after record."

Green wrote this decades ago. What would he say today? What he laments, however, may be inherent within the ethos itself. Celebrity and self-aggrandizement will always be a danger when pop culture, with its irreducible commercial agenda, is a driving force in music selected and performed for worship.

British pastor, John Blanchard in his little book *Pop Goes the Gospel* says this worldly exhibitionism sets up Christians to act like "stars instead of servants." He argues that the entertainment model inevitably leads to a groping for celebrity status and is why entertainment evangelism "so easily encourages worldliness."

What historian Paul Johnson observed about culture in general the Church seems desperate to imitate: "Entertainment [has] displaced traditional culture as the focus of attention, and celebrity has ejected quality as the measure of value."

THE LORD OF PEACE

How do we make peace when the other side just refuses to agree with us? The only way peace can be had in worship and in our warring over worship, is as we return to the Prince of Peace, to the One who made peace through the blood of his cross. "Crown him the Lord of peace," wrote hymn writer Matthew Bridges, "… that wars may cease…"

In 2009, the Bond family was catapulted into an unexpected, unanticipated liturgical journey. It has been a journey that has taken us into many different churches, denominations, conferences held in many different places, hearing many different preachers and teachers-- and singing in worship in a variety of forms from contemporary hipster, super loud, I-can't-hear-anyone-singing-at-all services, to psalm-singing services without instruments.

I have decided preferences, and can argue my reasons with both Scripture and Church history to defend myself (usually very sinfully). I was told once that I needed to get out more often, that I didn't really know what was going on in the Church. However true that was when I was told this, it is no longer remotely the case.

In fits and starts, I have been discovering the solution, the only solution to the war. It's not first changing the other guys to agree with me. It's about reorienting my heart to the splendor of the gospel of Jesus Christ. As obvious as that sounds, I'm convinced that getting the main thing back as the main thing in worship is the only solution.

Gene Edward Veith, writing for *World Magazine,* concluded his review of a wide range of popular Christian materials: "So much of this Christian material says nothing about Jesus Christ." Hymnody centered on Christ will help keep the Church from defection from the gospel, and Christ-centered priorities in every part of worship, liturgy, preaching, music—being Christ-centered in everything we do will help move us from swaggering critics to agents of peace.

In my travels I have begun to observe some welcome changes in at least some parts of the contemporary church, changes that may help us redraw some of the battle lines in the war. The Young Restless and Reformed movement (YRR) appeared to be a fresh rediscovery of biblical, confessional, and historic theology—a warm and passionate rediscovery of Reformed soteriology, and expository preaching, centered on Christ and the free grace of the gospel. And all of these elements combined have been for some YRR churches the engine of substantive and effective evangelism of the neediest, most broken people in our cities.

34

I think in the late 90s when I was writing the first Mr. Pipes book, there was blatantly crass exploitation of entertainment music in worship to give them what they want and grow your church; it was like being at a Mary Kay convention to go to some of those churches. But the YRR crowd, employing a grunge, hipster version of the entertainment ethos appeared to be moving the new reformational changes in a more theologically substantive direction. I rejoiced at what I was seeing then, though there has been significant and discouraging unraveling of the early good done in some YRR churches. Sadly, some of these high-profile, celebrity leaders have proven to be merely more young (or wish they still were) and restless than Reformed.

Many of us comfortably ensconced in our denominational cave may be missing this. We may still be fighting the last decades' battles, engaged in a partially passé worship war. It's not entirely over, far from it, but the phenomenon to contend with is much more complicated than I (and Mr. Pipes) used to think.

EARPLUGS FOR THE SERMON

Let me illustrate. It's oddly normal in the hipster church to have ushers passing out earplugs as you go into the service (easier solution: just turn down the volume). It's going to be loud in there, really loud. This is the generation that leads the world in premature hearing loss. My late father-in-law came by his hearing loss honorably, by driving a tank in the army, and by a life of hard work on commercial construction sites. Today's young hipster may be getting his hearing loss at church.

But it struck me, while visiting a hipster church one Easter as I grabbed a handful of earplugs on my way into the dark inner sanctum, how in a growing number of once-Reformed and evangelical churches we ought to plug our ears to save our souls from sermons that distort the radical grace of the gospel. Forget the music side of the worship war for a moment. Cram the earplugs in during the sermon! (While delivering a version of this chapter as a key-note address at an Alliance of Church Musicians conference, it was at this point that several people got up and walked out).

While we wrangle over how loud and raucous their music is, some hipster churches are passionate about proclaiming the free grace of the gospel of Jesus to the lost and broken world around us. At best, these churches are going into the highways and byways and compelling the outcasts, the misfits, those sometimes neglected by the more traditional churches, to come in, hear the good news and be saved.

I AM ONE OF THEM

I want to be thrilled with any church that is both believing, practicing, and faithfully proclaiming the gospel of Jesus Christ; all the better when these churches begin to rediscover that Reformed theology has been doing this for 500 years. Let's not stand on the sidelines, lobbing grenades at our brothers for their lousy music while they're being significantly used of God evangelizing the least of these.

Let's look at what those grenades look like; what do we often say about them? It's just hyped-up emotionalism, not real worship with the mind (some like being called cerebral Christians). Sure, it looks like joy, but it's just artificial, lacking in reverence and solemnity.

But is solemnity the most accurate quality for measuring acceptable worship? Some insist it is. As much as we must recover awe and reverence in worship, I wonder if that equates to solemnity. The psalmist makes me doubt that solemnity is the measure. "Then our mouth was filled with laughter, and our tongue with shouts of joy; then they said among the nations, 'The Lord has done great things for them'" (126:2).

Why so full of rejoicing? Why must we be so joyful in worship? Why make so much noise so joyfully?

Early in my adult life, I was a commercial photographer, working for magazines, corporations, medical industry, shipping, and I had a university client. While setting up lights and equipment for a photo shoot in a university classroom, I heard singing down the hall, singing of the praise chorus, worship song variety, energetic and happy.

"That's the only place on this campus," snorted the marketing director, "where those kids don't have to think." What followed were mocking and derisive comments from the art director, the registrar, and the student and faculty subjects for the shoot, leveled at the Intervarsity ministry and any student stupid enough to participate in it. The students continued singing. I continued setting up my gear and making test shots. Their intolerant rant continued. I stopped. Though it could jeopardize future work, I felt compelled to speak. "I'm one of them," I said. Awkward silence followed. I resumed my preparations. An hour or so later, after the shoot, while I put away my gear, the registrar came up and apologized. "I tried being a Christian once," he said. "It just didn't take." We talked.

This episode offered me two roads. Keep silent and do my job, and thereby passively align with the shameless mocking of the sophisticated university staff who had hired me, or align with a room full of college kids singing the praises of Jesus. They were choruses with little depth and had significant theological components missing. God made the road clear. I want to align with his people, whatever stage they are in their grasp of the riches of Christian worship and singing. "I am one of them."

SOLEMNITY OR JOY

I want to be like Augustine, listening in on the singing of the early church: "How greatly did I weep in thy hymns and canticles, deeply moved by the voices of thy Church so sweetly singing."

Or like John Bunyan while yet an unbeliever, eavesdropping on four Christian women chatting at their laundry. "They spake as if joy did make them speak," he recorded, and later immortalized them as the four virtuous women at House Beautiful.

I doubt that Augustine or Bunyan would have been overly impressed eavesdropping on solemnity. I believe we must recover awe and reverence in our corporate worship, but if our solemnity is not the prelude to overflowing joy at the grace of God in Jesus, it may simply be a caricature of reverence. Dour formalism can pass for solemnity for some of us, so can sophisticated detachment, boredom. Even depression could pass for solemnity.

Both joy and solemnity can be faked and have their counterfeits. Wise, self-aware Christians will ask themselves the hard question: Which pole am I most prone to? We see the ecstasy of the other guys and call it fake joy, superficial, unsophisticated. They see our solemnity and call it dead formalism, boredom, spiritual rigor mortis. Sometimes we're right and sometimes we are not.

Which one is retained when the Church shifts from caring about the authority of the Bible to caring more for the authority of new cultural ideas? The liberal progressive church that long ago abandoned the gospel of Martin Luther and the Reformers, still retains much of the appearance of reverence and solemnity in its worship services.

I'm frequently in European cathedrals, abbeys, and parish churches, most of them hollow shells of their former theological distinctives. But even though they have abandoned their spiritual convictions, in their formal gatherings, they retain the façade of reverence and solemnity. For most of us, solemnity is far easier to fake than real joy. Pharisees were great at solemnity in their worship.

We are in grave danger when we consider ourselves to have more in common with the progressive liberal church because of music style than we consider ourselves to have with churches that are passionate about the gospel and yet, at this stage in their understanding, use the entertainment ethos and pop contemporary music.

What will make the nations say, "The Lord has done great things for them"? Is it, "Wow! Look how solemn they are." No! It's joy, "shouts of joy" in our worship.

The elitist, power-monger critics of Calvin's ministry and the Reformation sneered at vernacular psalm singing, calling their songs "Geneva gigues." There's a reason why they didn't call them "Geneva dirges." Gigues melodies were joyful dance music for the common peasant. Clearly, Calvin's critics wanted more solemnity not more joy in Geneva's sung worship.

HEAVENLY ANTHEM

The Devil is, no doubt, elated over all this. Here we are in the very act of worship thinking we are better than other Christians and churches who don't do it our way. He is giddy, beside himself with glee.

Let's switch that exuberance around. We will be compelled to "sing to the Lord with cheerful voice" when our singing springs inexorably from gazing upon the beauty of Christ. When we sing because we are so bedazzled by the stupendous glory of Christ in the gospel, then, and then only, will the war cease, battle over. We will be so entirely smitten with wonder at who Jesus is and just what he has fully accomplished in our place in the gospel of free grace, that singing in worship will flow from the deep well of transformed hearts, minds, and tongues. Overwhelmed by the person and work of Christ, we can join our hearts and lips in sung worship of the Savior in ways that will lavish love and generosity on those with whom we differ.

Only when we love, not only our neighbor, but our Christian brethren, yes, even the ones who vastly

40

disagree with us on how we sing in worship, only then will the war be finished.

How we worship matters. But why we worship matters still more, and the fact that we worship with people from every tribe, kindred, people and tongue, matters first and last. Joyful singing because we have come more to love as we have first been loved by Christ—this matters above all.

Hymn writer Matthew Bridges thrills our hearts and joyfully invites us to join him in such a heavenly anthem:

> Crown him with many crowns,
> The Lamb upon his throne.
> Hark! How the heavenly anthem drowns
> All music but its own.

Weary of in-house warfare, together let us long for the day when "the heavenly anthem" does, indeed, "drown all music but its own." But we must tune our hearts, our minds, and our ears to what such a heavenly anthem would sound like. Such an anthem will be high above us, out of our reach, and will require "all that is within us." Surely, such an anthem must be closest to how God himself sings, closest to the psalms, closest to the hymn Jesus, the Prince of Peace, and his disciples sang at the Last Supper.

> Crown him the Lord of peace,
> Whose power a scepter sways;
> From pole to pole, that wars may cease,
> Absorbed in prayer and praise.

The more enthralled we are with the Redeemer, the more we are truly "absorbed in prayer and praise" of the "Lord of peace," the sooner our worship wars will cease.

All hail, Redeemer, hail!
For thou has died for me;
Thy praise shall never, never fail
Throughout eternity.

Let's recommit ourselves to singing the way God sings and the way we will be singing "throughout eternity."

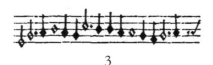

3

SING A NEW SONG

I f it was good enough for Isaac Watts, it's good enough for me." Few of us would come right out and say this, but I confess to thinking along those lines. Over two decades of writing and speaking about singing and liturgy, I've been accused of being a liturgical traditionalist. Skim through the proliferation of lyrics mass-produced in recent decades, and, whatever your particular taste in music, it's impossible not to observe how different they are from the psalms and hymns the Church has been singing for centuries. That's precisely by design. They were written not only to be different, but to be better, more relevant, to conform to a new ethos.

Some years ago, while visiting a church on our family vacation, we were invited to rise and sing the following:

You are my wholeness,
You are my completeness.
In you I find forgiveness,
Yes, in you I find release.

It's a wonder you take all those blunders I make
And so graciously offer me peace.

Bewildered, I reread the lines. Unless I was missing something, it appeared that the writer of these words had managed to flip everything around. The eternal living God who made the earth, the sky, the sea, and all that in them is, had been reduced to a means of individual self-discovery, "you are my completeness," the added bauble that finally makes me whole, as if God were a fashion accessory that puts the finishing touch on my outfit.

I looked around the congregation. Hands were raised; eyes were pinched shut with emotion. What was I missing? There were references to forgiveness and peace, vague ones, but blunders? Only those "who think of sin but lightly" will refer to their offences as blunders. The psalmist uses no such reductionist terminology. "Against you, you only, have I sinned and done what is evil in your sight" (51:4). To my ear, the flouncy cadence of the lines about blunders sounded so different from the earnest sobriety of David on his face confessing his evil to a holy God.

But, surely, this song had to get better. How could it get worse?

And in you I find true friendship,
Yes, your love is so free of demands,
Though it must hurt you so,
You keep letting me go
To discover the person I am.

44

Maybe I was being too critical, and the lyricist was onto a deeper truth in the line, "your love is so free of demands." I wanted to be more generous, find at least a morsel of truth that might redeem these lines.

While I cast about, I tried to picture the persecuted church singing this; imagine Christian martyrs throughout the centuries lustily joining in with "your love is so free of demands" as the fagots were lit beneath their feet at the stake. Not only was it nonsensical, singing this made a mockery of the persecuted church, then and now. Isaac Watts put it far better: "Love, so amazing, so divine/Demands my soul, my life, my all."

It felt like the fabricator of this ditty of self-actualization had learned his theology from a pop-psychology textbook—not from the Word of God. Truth and the honor of Christ were at stake. I looked down the pew at my family; we all stopped singing.

Historically, the finest poetry woos us away from self-absorption and makes us less self-referential. The best poetry "turn(s) us from ourselves to thee," as one poet put it. The Christian's chief end is to do all things to the glory of God alone; how much more so when we are taking poetic words on our lips, addressing God in sung worship?

Though we were no longer giving voice to these words, the rest of the congregation dutifully murmured onward:

And like a father you long to protect me,
Yet you know I must learn on my own.
Well, I made my own choice,
To follow your voice,

45

Guiding me unto my home.

Impotent and passive, the father figure portrayed by this lyricist now sits wringing his hands and waiting. How vastly different this is from the God of the Bible: "I am God, and there is none like me, declaring the end from the beginning and from ancient times things not yet done, saying, 'My counsel shall stand, and I will accomplish all my purpose'" (Isaiah 46:9-10). How equally dissimilar this is from the God portrayed in the rich canon of the Church's hymnody.

The final plumage of self-praise in "You Are My Wholeness" shifted to praising the songwriter's own choice. Unwittingly, all those who sing these words are praising themselves for following someone's voice. We're left to fill in many gaps, including who this someone is. Though the Apostle Paul calls us to do everything in the name of Jesus Christ (Colossians 3:17), oddly, while ostensibly singing to him, there is zero mention of the triune God, Father, Son, or Holy Spirit, in this reductionist doggerel.

Wouldn't ruined sinners rescued by Christ want to sing more like this?

Why was I made to hear thy voice,
And enter while there's room,
When thousands make a wretched choice,
And rather starve than come?

SING A NEW SONG

Hence, I confess, because of lyrics like "You Are My Wholeness," I had retreated into traditionalism. There's so many great psalm versifications and hymns to sing, let's solve the problem. Instead of being subjected to such unworthy lyrical nonsense, let's simply stick with the best of the past. I thought I'd found my safe place in self-righteous traditionalism.

Until reading in Psalms. I love singing Psalms, and I've always tried to avoid debate with my exclusive-psalm-singing brethren. "Oh, you only sing Psalms?" *Only*? The Psalms are the very words God breathed by his Spirit to the ancient poets who penned them. There's nothing *only* about them. But it was throughout those very psalms that I was repeatedly called to sing a new song (33, 40, 96, 98, 144, 149). As the psalms were once new expressions of praise for old covenant deliverances, so new manifestations of the gracious deliverance of our God call for new "songs of loudest praise" to give voice and substance to our new covenant gratitude.

But it wasn't just in Psalms. In Revelation the saints and angelic hosts, in a culminating torrent of splendor "…sang a new song, saying, 'Worthy are you to take the scroll and to open its seals, for you were slain, and by your blood you ransomed people for God from every tribe and language and people and nation'" (5:9). My traditionalism was getting pummeled.

THE MOUTHS OF BABES

Meanwhile, my children began to work on me. "Daddy, don't read us another book. Tell us a story, one you make up yourself." I pointed to the walls of books in our home. There are so many wonderful things to read. "No, Daddy, make up a story." That was twenty years ago. I've been making up stories ever since, my children often my chief critics. But writing books was one thing. Attempting to write a new hymn terrified me.

Then, I hit on a solution. I would have a character in one of my children's books (*The Accidental Voyage*) write a hymn. Throughout the story, my protagonist gnawed his pencil in fits and starts. It was perfect. If he managed to craft a poem that resembled a singable hymn, I was safe. More likely, if my efforts in his persona were an unmitigated disaster, I simply blamed the adolescent protagonist. What do you expect from a twelve-year-old? I felt liberated and furiously worked in secret on several other hymns. But exposure was around the corner.

After writing a birthday sonnet for a pastor friend of mine, he asked me to write a new hymn for the Thanksgiving service—in a week. His was a discerning congregation of hymn-savvy Presbyterians. What did he think I was, a performing circus animal able to crank out poetry that would stand up to their scrutiny? I declined.

Besides, my father, after a long battle with cancer, had recently died. I didn't feel much like writing a new hymn. We had sung hymns at my father's bedside, recited and sang psalms, the thirty-fourth emerging as one of his favorites. "This poor man cried to you and you delivered him out of all his trouble." He would often ask me to read it, then lean back on his pillow, close his eyes, and smile as I read.

Though I had declined to write the hymn, I found myself looking up biblical passages on thanksgiving, always drawn back to my father's favorite Psalm and the phrase, "O, taste and see that the Lord is good." I was thrilled with the Eucharist and Lord's Supper implications of the text. But the days before the Thanksgiving service were clicking by and all I had was an initial idea. Neophyte muse that I was, how could I possibly write a hymn in so short a time, one that would be worthy of the high worship of God?

Three days before the Thanksgiving service, I managed to produce five stanzas that began like this:

> We rise and worship you, our Lord,
>> With grateful hearts for grace outpoured,
> For you are good—O taste and see—
>> Great God of mercy rich and free.

The next stanzas explored the salvific roles of Father, Son, and Holy Spirit, for which every Christian has unmeasured cause for thanksgiving. To match the poetic meter, the accompanist had chosen a Long Meter existing tune. As the congregation rose, I sweated and fidgeted as we sang this new song.

HOSTILITY TO FORM

As Augustine put it, "I count myself among those who learn as they write and write as they learn." And did I ever need to learn several important things about hymns and writing them in these early efforts.

My poetry tutorials, however, began much earlier. God placed me in a hymn-singing, literary home, where we would snuggle up on the couch and listen to my mother read aloud from Shakespeare, even Chaucer in Middle English. Not understanding a word, I was charmed by the sounds and cadence of the poetry. In my adult life, during decades of teaching history and literature, including the writing of poetry, I watched with mounting apprehension as our culture descended further into a post-poetry, post-literacy malaise, the Church dutifully in tow.

Along with post-modernity's hostility to form, dismantling culture and disfiguring art, our ability to define and appreciate poetry has been marred. We're taught to disparage poetic conventions such as meter and rhyming, and anything else that gives shape and order to art. Literary experts say that we are to read poetry just like we read prose, as if poetry was a literary birth defect of prose rather than its own genre with its own rhetorical qualities.

For thousands of years, poetry has included various metrical patterns and parallelisms of sound, rhyming being one of the most delightful and anticipated. In our moment, however, *vers libre*, is celebrated as the highest form of poetry, emotive free verse that defies the conventions of the ages. With lines capriciously designated, much of this material is little more than fragmented prose masquerading as poetry.

Literary elites assure us that traditional poets were simply being cute with words, showing off, being crafty in their slavish devotion to convention. I wonder if they might also tell us that Michelangelo was just being crafty with marble, that medieval architects were simply showing off with stone-vaulted ceilings, or that J. S. Bach was merely being cute with counterpoint.

Critics of poetic conventions asked 20th century poet Robert Frost why he didn't write in free verse; he replied with an apt simile, "Writing poetry that doesn't rhyme is like playing tennis with the net down." Frost believed that there was something inherent in the genre that demanded structural boundaries if it is to be what it is. But his was a voice crying in a literary wilderness.

CONGREGATIONAL PASSIVITY

How does this relate to sung worship? Observe the congregation in a contemporary service, and it becomes clear that it is difficult to sing lyrics composed to post-poetry dictates. Throughout much of Western Civilization, poetry was composed to be sung by the whole clan. Today, singing is now largely done for us by commercially popular, celebrity entertainers, or those who imitate them. The congregation has become avid listeners, but increasingly inept participants in full-voice singing.

Finding myself a guest in many different churches, most arranged with the entertainers and their instruments on center stage, I've been observing congregational singing for years. Many people are not singing at all, especially the men, and most of those whose lips are moving, are murmuring more than full-voice singing. Why is that?

Whatever our playlists look like, and however lustily we might sing in the privacy of our cars, let's be frank, one who is not a pop musician feels uncomfortable attempting in public to sing like a solo-voice entertainer. It turns out, though they call themselves worship leaders, they are not leading us. They are doing it for us. Our participation is irrelevant to the performance. Join in if you care to; either way, it will not change the instrumental, high-volume sound pulsing through the worship center.

CONGREGATIONAL SINGING

So, how are we to write, compose, and sing new songs that reflect the ethos of worship rather than the ethos of entertainment? David played his harp, a solo performer—for the sheep. But he wrote psalms to be sung by the congregation, young and old, without any consideration for generational preferences. Hence, as we attempt to craft new songs, the hymn writer will not write for a solo performer or for a choir. A good hymn could be sung by either, but the writer of a new hymn, like David, will intentionally craft poetry accessible for the whole congregation of God's people to sing with full voice.

When Christians of all ages and various singing abilities rise to their feet to sing the praises of their Redeemer, if things are to be done decently and in order, they will want to sing with one voice. Though it is more difficult to observe when hymn poetry is subordinated to the musical score, as in American hymnals, for centuries, virtually all hymns have been written in regular rhyme and meter. Solo entertainers can sing metrically irregular songs, and often do, but singing free verse worship songs is difficult for the congregation.

WHAT MAKES A GOOD HYMN?

Our greatest problem discerning what is worthy to sing in worship is firstly a theological problem. Egalitarians don't make good worshipers. Sinners, undone by their crimes in the face of a holy God, falling on their faces before the Sovereign Lord who has paid their vast debt in full with his precious blood, make better worshippers. We must get our theology right before we can correct our doxology.

Another problem we have with evaluating what is worthy to sing in worship is that we no longer think of hymns as poetry, and in our post-poetry culture, we have lost the literary tools to require the highest standards for that poetry. What we sing before the face of our Redeemer in worship must be the finest human poetry, set to the most appropriate human music, shaped by the biblical ethos of worship.

Music in worship is not firstly about loud instruments, multi-colored lights, or soloists aping entertainment celebrities, as we see in the ubiquitous nightclub liturgy of our present situation. Music in worship is first and last about the voice of the congregation singing to and with one another the word of Christ. Paul put it this way:

> Let the word of Christ dwell in you richly as you teach and admonish one another with all wisdom, and as you sing psalms, hymns and spiritual songs with gratitude in your hearts to God. And whatever you do, whether in word or deed, do it all in the name of the Lord Jesus, giving thanks to God the Father through him (Colossians 3:16-17).

Here, Paul tells us how and what to sing. New songs of new covenant worship find their substance and boundaries in this *locus classicus* of sung worship. Notice, three times we are told to take Christ's name on our lips in our singing, and we're told three times in the whole context of the passage to sing our thanksgiving. Which strongly suggests that new lyrics will be Christ-centered and filled with gratitude.

The passage reveals three more functions of hymns, summarized by hymnologist Erik Routley: New covenant hymns will codify doctrine ("teach and admonish"), unify the Church ("one another"), and glorify God ("to God"). We have seen decay of all three of these functions in most of the new songs of recent decades. Praise choruses and worship songs have been generally reductionist in theological content, saying less and less about doctrinal truths, often never using the name of Christ.

Furthermore, instead of unifying the Church, the shift to lyrics and music that suit the ethos of entertainment, has created a generational rift, disunifying the Church. Some churches have a traditional service and a contemporary one, thus, dividing the congregation by tastes and age rather than bringing Christians together with one voice in song. A good test if a lyric will unify the Church is to ask if the persecuted church would choose to sing it; would the early church sing it; would Christians have sung it in the Reformation, the Great Awakening, or the Missionary Movement of the 19th century?

Lastly, the third function of singing to the glory of God been under attack for decades. When churches prefer singing what entertainers sing at concerts, or what Christian radio stations are playing, there is a pull to imitate the entertainment industry and its popular celebrity method of singing, church worship leaders now attempting to look like and sound like they are on stage at a concert.

The late Keith Green, himself a vanguard of contemporary Christian singing, was offended by the "'look at me!' attitude I have seen at concert after concert, and the 'Can't you see we are as good as the world!' syndrome" of fellow rock and roll performers. Decades later, would Green be less offended by what he would see were he alive today?

However noble the intentions, the entertainment arrangement is the perfect storm for singing to the glory of the performers on the stage. Routley quips that when the three functions of hymns, codify, unify, glorify, are absent, he wished for the song to have "the short life of all rootless things."

NEW REFORMATION HYMNS

Finally, Paul tells us to write and sing new hymns "with all wisdom," that is to do so skillfully; which means those who presume to craft new hymn lyrics or compose tunes for those lyrics need to study, develop their skills, know what they are attempting, stand on the shoulders of the great hymn writers of the past— Cowper, Watts, Wesley, Havergal, Bonar and many others.

It was while immersed in the study of our hymnody that I became so reluctant to attempt writing a new hymn. How could I possibly measure up with the best hymn writers of the past? Then it occurred to me: I don't write books because I think I'm the best writer in the world, any more than I love my wife because I think I'm the best husband in the world, any more than I parent my kids because I think I'm the best parent in the world, any more than I worship Christ because I think I'm the best worshiper in the world. Neither do I write hymns because I think I'm the best hymn writer in the world.

Then, one frosty December evening, as I scribbled in front of the fire, I found myself toying with the idea of attempting a carol. When I came to my senses, I contemplated tossing my notes into the fire. What was I thinking? Christ's Advent? The sacred mystery? Angelic heralds? The culmination of thousands of years of prophecy? The best of the existing carol canon guaranteed failure. Carols are uniquely rich with celebratory atmosphere, evocative of rejoicing and feasting, sleigh bells, and every charming winter association imaginable. Hymnologists tell us the best-loved hymn of all time is actually a carol, Charles Wesley's "Hark, the Herald Angels Sing." It was literary suicide to attempt a carol.

Because of my fears, early scribblings for this carol lay dormant for several years; hymn writing can sometimes be like that for me, an initial burst of ideas, then nothing, just an imaginative black hole. And then another Advent season approached. I read aloud from Luke's gospel with my family; we sang a carol. When the kids were tucked in their beds, I pulled out my initial notes and sifted through the scribbled idea banks and word banks. Late that night, with fear and trembling, I managed to set down six stanzas as they appear below, beginning with the angelic announcement of Christ's Advent to the shepherds, proceeding to our Lord's sinless life, Gethsemane and the cross, the resurrection, concluding with Christ's triumphant Second Advent.

What wonder filled the starry night

When Jesus came with heralds bright!
I marvel at his lowly birth,
    That God for sinners stooped to earth.

His splendor laid aside for me,
    While angels hailed his Deity,
The shepherds on their knees in fright
    Fell down in wonder at the sight.

The child who is the Way, the Truth,
    Who pleased his Father in his youth,
Through all his days the Law obeyed,
    Yet for its curse his life he paid.

What drops of grief fell on the site
    Where Jesus wrestled through the night,
Then for transgressions not his own,
    He bore my cross and guilt alone.

What glorious Life arose that day
    When Jesus took death's sting away!
His children raised to life and light,
    To serve him by his grace and might.

One day the angel hosts will sing,
    "Triumphant Jesus, King of kings!"
Eternal praise we'll shout to him
    When Christ in splendor comes again!

4

WHAT DIFFERENCE DOES IT MAKE

Why hat do you do for a living?" the barista asked the twenty-something-looking young man waiting for his Venti-Iced-Skinny-Hazelnut-Macchiato, Sugar-Free-Syrup, Extra-Shot, No-Whip coffee.

His reply? "I write worship songs. I write worship songs. I write worship songs."

All right, I realize there's an entire generation of people who not only don't think that's funny, they no longer have a comparative context out of which to understand where it even came from. For them, 7-11 songs are what's playing on the music loop at a convenience store chain.

Try introducing the poetry of Isaac Watts to students even at a Christian school, and someone will raise his hand and ask what everyone else was thinking. "Wait, didn't Watts invent the steam engine? Why are we studying him in literature class?"

HOW VAST THE DIFFERENCE

What's the difference between what the Church has been singing for nearly 2,000 years and what the Church is singing in the last few decades? To be more specific, what is the difference between what Theodulph of Orleans wrote in 821 and the proliferation of new material composed in less than half a century? Theodulph wrote:

> All glory, laud and honor,
> To thee, Redeemer, King,
> To whom the lips of children
> Made sweet hosannas ring.
>
> Thou art the king of Israel,
> Thou David's royal Son,
> Who in the Lord's name comest,
> The King and Blessèd One...

Rooted in Scripture and redemptive history, this infectious poem transports us to Jesus' triumphal entry into Jerusalem where the crowds, even children, "made sweet hosannas ring." Theodulph of Orleans opens our ears; we can hear them singing. Assisted by the translator, able English poet John Mason Neale, we are drawn in; more than anything, we want to join in the "glory, laud, and honor." We want our lips to ring with the royal names of Jesus. And congregations of Christ's Church have been doing so for 1,300 years since.

Fast forward to the present moment in redemptive history. Let's hold this thrilling medieval hymn up to the things the Church has been singing in the last few decades. How does this worship song attributed to Jesus Culture measure up? Brace yourself.

> Higher than the mountains that I face
> Stronger than the power of the grave
> Constant through the trial and the change
> One thing remains
> This one thing remains
> Your love never fails, and never gives up
> It never runs out on me
> Your love never fails, and never gives up
> It never runs out on me
> Your love never fails, and never gives up
> It never runs out on me...

It reminds me of old technology, when the vinyl record got scratched and the needle just couldn't, just couldn't, just couldn't get past the scratch. We wish the lyricist would just stop. Though he obviously has so very little to say, he does not let that deter him; he bungles on, over and over again, saying very little about no one in particular.

But some might object. "You've picked out the worst song of the genre." Be assured; it is not. There are many more like it and worse. In fairness, there are others that are better, but they are precisely better as they move away from contemporary singing priorities and more toward the content and structure of the hymnody of the centuries.

So, what is the difference between centuries of Christian singing and the songs of the last decades?

SKILL AND ZEAL

The first great difference has to do with the skill and experience of the men and women who wrote them.

Though educational elites insist that it is not so, great literature is timeless and universal because it speaks throughout the ages to everyone in every condition of life. Nowhere is this more perfectly seen than in the Psalms. Penned under Divine inspiration, it's little wonder the Psalms are the gold standard by which all other lyric must be measured. In his *Reflections on the Psalms*, C. S. Lewis declared Psalm 19 "one of the greatest lyrics in the world." Even unbelievers who reject the unique divine origins of the Psalms, admit that it's some of the finest poetry ever penned. What is it about the Psalms? C. H. Spurgeon offers an explanation based on the breadth of experience of their principal author:

> David knew the trials of all ranks and conditions of men. Kings have their troubles, and David wore a crown; the peasant has his cares, and David handled a shepherd's crook; the wanderer has many hardships, and David abode in the caves of Engedi; ...The psalmist was also tried in his friends... "he that eateth bread with me, hath lifted up his heel against me." His worst foes were they of his own household... David no sooner escaped from one trial than he fell into another, no sooner emerged from one season of despondency and alarm, than he was again brought into the lowest depths, and all God's waves and billows rolled over him.

David's psalms are universally the delight of experienced Christians. Whatever our frame of mind, whether ecstasy or depression, David has exactly described our emotions. He was an able master of the human heart…

This wide-ranging breadth of skill and experience of David and the psalmists qualified these men for their poetic task.

Correspondingly, the vast majority of 2,000 years of Christian hymnody was penned by poets with extensive literary experience and training, both formal and informal. St. Andrew of Crete (660-732), for example, the poet who wrote "Christian Dost Thou See Them," not only had formal literary training, he was a teacher of literature. Until only very recently, education centered around literature, and literature was almost entirely poetry. Hence, both Theodulph and Andrew, and The Venerable Bede ("A Hymn of Glory Let Us Sing"), Bernard of Clairvaux ("O Sacred Head, Now Wounded"), Ambrose of Milan ("O Trinity, Most Blessed Light"), Prudentius ("Of the Father's Love Begotten"), and many other hymn writers of the early centuries, were skillful writers. They had mastered all the subtleties and nuances of poetic imagery and cadence.

Fast forward to the last forty years. Herein lies one of the great differences. The vast majority of worship songs, and praise choruses were written by musicians, usually young guitar players, often new converts, with no shortage of enthusiasm and zeal for the gospel. However much formal musical training they've had, most have had little or no formal literary experience and training. They are musicians first who've learned songwriting by listening to and then imitating their favorite pop bands from the last few decades.

Furthermore, while the centuries of poets writing the Church's hymnody began first with words, lines, stanzas, written with goosequill and ink on parchment, many contemporary lyrics emerged after and subordinate to the chords plucked out on the guitar strings. They were first musical sounds; as the composition began to take shape, almost as an afterthought, words were added, worship-esque-sounding words.

Notice another and far more important difference between the writers of our hymnody and the crafters of contemporary worship songs. Over the centuries, it was largely mature Christians, most with theological training and years of studying their Bibles, many were pastors and pastors' wives, who wrote our best and most enduring hymnody. Conversely, most contemporary worship songs were written by young, zealous musicians with little or no theological training.

Frankly, it's not fair to compare them. Though full of zeal, the modern songwriter falls so far short of the literary and theological caliber of their historical predecessors it is absurd to compare them. But there is one enormous advantage the songwriter has, one they lean heavily upon and exploit to its maximum capabilities. Their advantage is the entertainment ethos with all of its glitter and volume. Who needs literary skill and theological understand when you have bright lights and loud sounds? And voice enhancement technology to tidy up the worship leader's voice so he or she can sound more like the popular entertainers who originally recorded the song they are regurgitating in the thinly veiled guise of congregational singing.

SUBSTANCE OVER SENTIMENT

There are other important differences that will be elaborated throughout this book, but the following is a brief comparison of the songs the Church has been singing for two millennia and what we've been singing for four or five decades.

Hymns of praise give objective and theological reasons for the praise, while many modern songs merely make statements of praise and restatements, repeated over and again. In the recent material, there is little or no adorning of the truth stated, little showing of the beauty of holiness, which is so very unlike the psalms and great hymns of the centuries. This is no small omission.

Psalms and hymns are Godward, vertical, concerned with the attributes and works of God. Conversely, recent songs tend to be more about the experience of the singer, horizontal, subjective, and often sentimental.

Worship songs are usually not modeled on the biblical Psalms, not in any depth, like the best hymns, but are modeled on what fits with the popular entertainment sounds.

Hymn writers wrote for the human voice to sing, and the music was composed to aid the voice of the congregation in singing. Contemporary worship songs tend to be dominated by musical instruments and the high-volume of the music rather than the voice of the congregation.

Hymns, like psalms, have stood the test of time, because they were crafted to be enduring, to be accessible to the human condition in every generation. The recent songs are shaped by what is popular now, which is always going to be transient, in vogue, out of vogue.

While many psalms and hymns are prayers offered directly to God, many new songs are lyrically circular, and place the worshipper in the rather awkward posture of singing to ourselves about what we're singing about.

Of supreme importance, the best of our historic hymnody is Christological, including versified psalms that feature their fulfillment in Christ. Oddly, many of the new songs, composed ostensibly for evangelism, never get around to naming Christ. Instead, many song writers just use second-person pronouns that could be anybody, reducing corporate worship to singing vague love songs to nobody in particular.

SOLOISTS ON THE STAGE

One of the most awkward qualities of many worship songs is that they were first composed for a solo voice, usually the lead vocalist in a band. In the church service, the worship leader becomes the lead vocalist, usually attempting to make his voice sound like the pop entertainer's voice who first popularized the new song. This can be difficult, even entirely inaccessible, for untrained voices of the congregation to imitate. Allow me to switch from popular to higher-culture singing to illustrate the point.

Imagine trying to sing like Luciano Pavarotti, the "king of the high C's" as he was known. Imagine him leading worship. Imagine trying to follow his booming tenor. Though he was one of the greatest tenors of all time, and could do astounding things with his highly trained instrument, his voice, almost nobody in the congregation has the capability to follow his leading. We would be inclined not to sing. We would want to listen, not mess up his performance. What is more, we would be wholly embarrassed to attempt to sing like an opera singer. Our neighbors would think we were putting on an affected manner of singing. They would be correct.

Whether we appreciate opera or not, even those of us who do, do not think it would be appropriate to try to make our congregational singing sound like Francis Poulenc's *Dialogues of the Carmelites*.

But that brings up the question: Why is it that we have wholly embraced the popular entertainer's voice and ethos but not an opera singer's ethos? Why would it be inappropriate and unworkable to pattern our corporate worship singing after the music in Handel's *Messiah,* or Mendelssohn's *Elijah*?

Though pop entertainers are aiming at an entirely different vocal objective, it is, nevertheless, one that is highly specialized, requires a stage full of props, has its required conventions, though these are transient and based on the latest new bands and ever-evolving popular genres. But popular entertainment singing is not singing in the normal human fashion. We must be conditioned by popular entertainers to sing or attempt to sing the way they do.

CHILDREN SINGING

One of my granddaughters as a two-year-old heard opera and thereafter for months she attempted to use her version of vibrato whenever she sang anything—which was often. It was hilarious. None of us could keep a straight face when she did it.

Children don't naturally use vibrato or croon and cavort when they sing unless they have been conditioned to do so by loads of screen time watching entertainers do that kind of performance singing. Without the entertainment conditioning, however, children just sing: clear, joyful, unaffected singing. It whelms up from within them as image bearers of God. Their singing often can be full-voice, uninhibited, unaffected singing, like God sings, rejoicing over his children with loud singing (Zephaniah 3:17).

While God's singing would make Pavarotti sound like a novice, hearing God singing would make us want to sing with him and like him. Far from intimidating us into silence, God, who exults over us with loud singing, made us for singing, calls us to sing back to him, to sing with him, to make a joyful noise unto him with our instrument, our voice.

The overwhelming evidence suggests that the typical worship leader, however well-intentioned, is not even striving to awaken the congregation's instrument. Keith Getty urges worship leaders to self-assess after worship: "How well did our congregation sing? Our role is simply to be an accompaniment to them as they sing."

Accompanying the human voice ought to be the principle thing any worship leader is doing. Whatever instruments are used to accompany the singing (not all instruments are as well suited to this role as others), it ought to be the objective of musicians to create an environment whereby the congregation's voice will be heard above all other sounds in the room. God-honoring worship leaders will be like C. S. Lewis's London cabby: "Stop your noise," they will say to any sounds that compete with the voice of the congregation as it teaches and admonitions one another in corporate sung worship.

But it is not like that in the average contemporary worship service. It is far more the reverse. It sometimes seems as if the band is saying to the congregation, "Stop your noise," listen to my guitar, this cool riff, this clever bridge, my drums, my keyboard. Murmur along if you'd like to, but what's most important here, is us and our instrumental music.

Music in many churches has become yet another concert, the gathering of God's people on the Lord's Day merely another venue for that concert. The band has been practicing for the concert all week, and hopes you enjoy it. As at many concerts, you may even join in on some of your favorites, but don't mess up the performance.

Subverted by the entertainment ethos, the chancel becomes a stage on which a performance occurs for the pleasure or amusement of the audience—who are welcome to applaud after we're done. Whatever other context where this kind of performance might be appropriate, it's awkwardly conjoined, at best, with the vertical nature of Christian worship.

FOLK MUSIC FOR FOLKS

If solo entertainment music, pop or classical, are difficult for the congregation to emulate, what genre remains?

Perhaps it's music composed by folks for folks to sing. Folk music from many different traditions is far more accessible to the normal singing experience of untrained musicians and singers. Perhaps this is why so many of the most enduring hymn tunes have come from German, Scandinavian, English, Welsh, African-American Spiritual, and Irish folk music traditions.

One of the great strengths of Stuart Townend's 2001 hymn lyric "In Christ Alone" is that it was set to a melody composed by Irishman Keith Getty. "Being brought up [in Ireland]," said Getty, "gave me a sense of melody that is very attuned to congregational singing."

Whatever our ethnic upbringing, something resonates in the human soul with the ancient Irish folk tune *Slane* when we sing "Be Thou My Vision." It needs no tampering. The timeless melody perfectly supports the rich lyric. The music compels us—not merely to clap, sway, and listen—but to sing, really sing, with full heart and voice, and minds wholly engaged.

Not all musical styles can do that. Many were never intended to do so. Is it even possible to begin with pop performance music that was produced for a multi-billion-dollar industry and then expect it to work for congregational singing?

Appetites for music change over time, and the changes are usually driven by philosophical and moral agendas. The musical style that takes center stage in most churches today was produced in the last fifty years as both outgrowth and catalyst to the sexual revolution of what Paul Johnson called "the decadent decade," the 1960s. I state that not as opinion but as manifest fact. The sexual revolution did not produce polka music; it produced rock and roll, and its derivations, including middle-of-the-road pop music, as employed in most churches.

Though not a fan of T. S. Eliot's poetry, I find his cultural prognostications uniquely perceptive. As a publicist he was constantly observing cultural changes and had this to say about the shift to what was popular in his day, a world on the cusp of the "decadent decade."

> Pop entertainment is a purely commercial enterprise, an imitation and perversion of folk culture. It is addictive but transitory, appealing to an appetite for novelty and distraction. Pop entertainment is truly the opiate of the masses in a leveling society: numbing, anesthetic, escapist.

If Eliot is at all correct, we are forced to ask ourselves: How can the eternal, unchangeable truths of the gospel be communicated in a transitory medium that appeals to listeners' love of novelty, escapism, and distraction, that numbs them and anesthetizes them? Eliot proceeds to contrast pop entertainment as a perversion of folk culture which "is enduring, noncommercial, and anonymous, and it is perpetuated by families, schools, and clubs. It unifies the members of a local community, living, dead, and not yet born, a source of collective memory."

He should have added, "and churches." If Eliot is at all right, which one is most suited to congregational singing in Christian worship? Which one unifies, perpetuates, endures, encourages us collectively to remember? If "Pop entertainment is a purely commercial enterprise," as Eliot insists, and as a cursory glance at the CCM industry discloses, it because ingenuous in the extreme to sing:

> Riches I heed not, nor man's empty praise,
> Thou mine Inheritance, now and always:
> Thou and thou only, first in my heart,
> High King of Heaven, my Treasure thou art.

Singing these words surrounded by an ethos scripted by the multi-billion-dollar entertainment industry—the stage arrayed with glitz and glitter, high-tech volume pulsing throughout the worship center—may prove to be far more than merely a "perversion of folk culture."

5

C. S. LEWIS'S DISLIKE OF HYMNS

A generation ago, most mature Christians knew the power of singing psalms and psalm-like hymns in worship, in the home, and around the family table. Experienced Christians knew more of life and of the reality of death; they had knelt at the deathbed of loved ones and friends, and made the connection. A disciplined life of joyful singing was one of the very important ways we prepared ourselves for singing in the hour of death, blessing and encouraging the dying—and ourselves, the bereaved living.

Enter one of the great tragic problems for the new generation of Christians who have spent their lives singing happy-clappy songs, with little or nothing about death and dying in those songs, and singing them in a venue that requires the full array of entertainment instruments and soloists to lead us, a venue that is wholly inaccessible at the deathbed. There'll be no band, no lead vocalist, nor will there be an organ at your loved one's deathbed—or at yours.

Thoughtful Christians, ones who look down the road, will want to sing in the home and in their churches in ways that can be portable, can be carried on in the hospice bed. Christian, rediscover how to sing, before it's too late.

The stories are legion of the elderly unable to remember anything and anyone, but able to sing hymns they had learned in their childhood. My father-in-law, suffering with Alzheimer's, unable to remember his own wife and children, and unable to read the words in front him, sang Christmas carols with us a few short months before his death, all by memory—which he had of nothing else. Ten minutes before my father died, he sang Psalm 23 with us; I believe he was even harmonizing on the bass line, as he had taught me to do in corporate singing as a young man.

But it's not just the elderly. There's the 2014 account of eighteen-year-old Lexi Hansen who was pronounced brain dead and on life support after being struck by a car while riding her longboard. The doctors were grim; they said the unresponsive teen had a 5% likelihood of survival. Lexi's mother gave the account of the family joining hands around her hospital bed, expecting her to die. Then, one of them began singing hymns. The rest of the family joined in. In moments, Lexi's eyes opened, and she squeezed her family's hands as they sang.

I remember seeing my aunt who had turned away from her Christian upbringing, now in her eighties, weeping as we stood around the piano singing hymns from her childhood, hymns whose content she no longer claimed to believe. Tears, nevertheless.

In his *Confessions*, Augustine credits overhearing Christians singing with preparing his heart for the gospel. "How greatly did I weep in thy hymns and canticles, deeply moved by the voices of thy Church so sweetly singing."

It would be impossible to overstate the role of corporate singing in the Reformation. John Calvin, cautious about music, nevertheless, knew its power over human hearts. "Music has a secret and almost incredible power to move hearts." And Luther ranked music, and singing hymns together in worship, next only to the Word of God and theology.

SOLITARY CONCEIT

Though C. S. Lewis did not get everything right, one of the things that compels many of us back to his writing, is that in the things he did get right he wrote and spoke about those things better than just about anyone. But when it comes to singing in corporate worship, Lewis seems unable to break free of some of his early prejudices against corporate singing. Put bluntly, Lewis did not agree with Augustine, Calvin, and Luther about hymns and the power of singing them in worship, at least not initially.

Picture Lewis as a new convert in 1931, knotting his tie and walking from his home The Kilns to attend corporate worship at Holy Trinity parish church for the very first time as a true believer in Christ, in working-class Headington Quarry, only three miles from the exalted spires of his sophisticated life at the oldest university in England, but an intellectual and aesthetic cosmos apart from his life in blue-color Headington Quarry.

In his collection of essays, *God in the Dock*, Lewis describes his initial impression of his neighbors' singing, their untrained voices, their unrefined musical tastes.

> I disliked very much their hymns, which I considered to be fifth-rate poems set to sixth-rate music. But as I went on, I saw the great merit of it. I came up against different people of quite different outlooks and different education, and then gradually my conceit just began peeling off. I realized that the hymns (which were just sixth-rate music) were, nevertheless, being sung with devotion and benefit by an old saint in elastic-side boots in the opposite pew, and then you realize that you aren't fit to clean those boots. It gets you out of your solitary conceit. It is not for me to lay down laws, as I am only a layman, and I don't know much.

Notice the development of his opinion about their singing, "the great merit of it." Whatever his claims about not knowing much, Lewis had finely tuned, refined musical and literary tastes. Literature was his life's work. He was one of the best-read scholars of his century, and much of that reading was poetry. Yet, he was operating under the cloud of postmodern changes in poetry, the Imagists of the early 20th century, the fragments of *vers libre* poets, and the general revolt against conventional poetry, the kind Lewis appreciated, understood, and loved. This may have had an influence on his early rejection of their "fifth-rate hymns." The literary elites of the 20th century insisted that poetry with specific theological content was lesser poetry, perhaps not even worthy of being included as poetry. Lewis could not be entirely unaffected by his culture's secular prejudice.

But observe Lewis's change, his confession that it was his pride, his "solitary conceit" that led to his early dislike of corporate singing at Holy Trinity.

HYMN TO EVOLUTION

More of a spoof than a true hymn of praise to God, Lewis did set his pen to write a hymn, a tongue-in-cheek lyric to evolution.

> Lead us, Evolution, lead us
> Up the future's endless stair;
> Chop us, change us, prod us, weed us.
> For stagnation is despair:
> Groping, guessing, yet progressing,
> Lead us nobody knows where.

Having fun at evolution's expense, Lewis continues his playfully derisive verse through several more stanzas. We can't help applauding his mocking lyric. But Lewis, of course, would not rank this as a proper hymn to be sung in the praise of God in corporate worship.

CORRUPT TEXTS

Nevertheless, hymns and singing not infrequently appear in Lewis's writing. I suspect he was being autobiographical at times in his magisterial *Screwtape Letters*. For instance, when he has his senior demon

Screwtape reveal his strategy for tempting the new convert., a new convert that sounds suspiciously like Lewis's revulsion on first attending corporate worship.

> One of our great allies at present is the Church itself. Do not misunderstand me. I do not mean the Church as we see her spread out through all time and space and rooted in eternity, terrible as an army with banners. That I confess, is a spectacle which makes our boldest tempters uneasy. But fortunately it is quite invisible to these humans. All your patient sees is the half-finished, sham Gothic erection on the new building estate. When he goes inside, he sees the local grocer with rather an oily expression on his face bustling up to offer him one shiny little book containing a liturgy which neither of them understands, and one shabby little book containing corrupt texts of a number of religious lyrics, mostly bad, and in very small print.

Put yourself in Lewis's place. British hymnals are often in very small print, hard to read in dim, old-world sanctuaries. And, true enough, far too many "corrupt texts" of inferior lyrics have been included in hymnals. Sentimental lyrics about coming to gardens alone, or repetitive revival songs that sound more like background music for the carousel would be repugnant to someone of Lewis's literary refinement. But he does admit that these "religious lyrics" are only "mostly bad," which suggests that he appreciated at least some of the lyrics that appeared in hymnals, as I will demonstrate in this chapter.

SINGING OUT OF TUNE

Not everyone has perfect pitch, or absolute pitch as musical experts term it. In fact, musicologists tell us only one in ten thousand people are blessed (or is it cursed?) with the ability to hear and sing in perfect pitch—and hear when anyone else is not. Nevertheless, those same musical experts tell us that the vast majority of those of us without absolute pitch have relative pitch, that is, the ability to recognize the note we are supposed to be singing and match our voice with it more or less closely. But have you ever stood next to someone in a worship service who falls in the category of being tone deaf, unable to match his voice to what most everyone else is singing?

I know a man who loves singing, but he is tone deaf—stone-cold, tone deaf. But, because he is, he can sing the praises of Jesus with abandon. He doesn't hear that his pitch is different from everyone else's, and so he throws his head back and sings with gusto, as well he should. God, the giver of all good gifts, and the withholder of the same, wants his people to sing loudly, like he sings over his beloved, even over the ones who can't carry a tune in a bucket.

Lewis must have found himself sitting near a fellow like that. He continues in *Screwtape Letters*:

> …When he gets to his pew and looks round him he sees just that selection of his neighbors whom he has hitherto avoided. You want to lean pretty heavily on those neighbors… You may know one of them to be a great warrior on the Enemy's side. No matter.

Your patient, thanks to Our Father Below, is a fool. Provided that any of those neighbors sing out of tune, or have boots that squeak, or double chins, or odd clothes, the patient will quite easily believe that their religion must therefore be somehow ridiculous.

FEWER, BETTER, AND SHORTER HYMNS

Though Lewis eventually saw through his "solitary conceit" at his first impressions of ordinary Christians gathering to sing in church, he would continue to speculate about the value of untrained corporate singing, "this noise," as he terms it. In his *Christian Reflections* he wrote:

> What we want to know is whether untrained communal singing is in itself any more edifying than other popular pleasures. And of this I, for one, am still wholly unconvinced. I have often heard this noise; I have sometimes contributed to it. I do not yet seem to have found any evidence that the physical and emotional exhilaration which it produces is necessarily, or often, of any religious relevance. What I, like many other laymen, chiefly desire in church are fewer, better, and shorter hymns; especially fewer.

I have had the privilege of meeting several people who knew Lewis, studied under him at Oxford, sat through lectures, and who worshiped at Holy Trinity with him. One man I met at St. Michael's, the City Church in Oxford, told me that he had been an active member at Holy Trinity for "as long as [he] could remember," and in his youth he had been a choir boy and remembers Mr. Lewis very well. "He did not care much for our singing," he said. He recalled that when the service was drawing to a close, just before the final anthem, Lewis and Warnie would slide out of their pew and beeline to the exit. This may have been as much to avoid small talk after the service, which he abhorred, as to avoid the "long roar" of congregational singing.

MUSIC AS A MEANS OF GRACE

In an essay entitled "On Church Music," included in Lewis's *Christian Reflections*, he makes a particularly relevant observation about two kinds of leaders of corporate worship, especially as it relates to music. Some things do not change. The tension between high church and low church music, or elitist and popular, or traditional and contemporary—however we term the opposing poles in the church music debate—there've likely been conflicts over music in worship for centuries. Though somewhat altruistic, Lewis here gives us the gracious perspective each side ought to have toward the other side:

> There are two musical situations on which I think we can be confident that a blessing rests. One is where a priest or an organist, himself a man of trained and delicate taste, humbly and charitably sacrifices his own (aesthetically right) desires and gives the people humbler and coarser fare than he would wish, in a belief (even, as it may be, the erroneous belief) that he can thus bring them to God. The other is where the stupid and unmusical

layman humbly and patiently, and above all silently, listens to music which he cannot, or cannot fully, appreciate, in the belief that it somehow glorifies God, and that if it does not edify him this must be his own defect. Neither such a High Brow nor such a Low Brow can be far out of the way. To both, Church Music will have been a means of grace; not the music they have liked, but the music they have disliked. They have both offered, sacrificed, their taste in the fullest sense.

Though there is much more to be said, here Lewis does give us pause. How many of us have cringed our way through singing that we found far lesser than what we felt God deserved from his people. Before long, for some of us that cringing turned to griping and criticizing, maybe devolving further into mocking and disparaging the intelligence or skill of the meat-headed musicians. On whichever side of the worship wars you take up your weapons, I suspect we've all done this, as Lewis so clearly had done.

Continuing his thoughts on high church and low church music, Lewis contrasts the two paths of blessing with their opposite:

But where the opposite situation arises, where the musician is filled with the pride of skill or the virus of emulation and looks with contempt on the unappreciative congregation (or on other churches and factions that don't align with his enlightened musical and liturgical views), or where the unmusical, complacently entrenched in their own ignorance and conservatism look with the restless and resentful hostility of an inferiority complex on all who would try to improve their taste – there, we may be sure, all that both offer is unblessed and the spirit that moves them is not the Holy Ghost.

UNBLESSED SPIRIT

Observe how this unblessed spirit Lewis describes can apply to the advocate for the higher beauties of artistic music or the champion of popular entertainment styles of music. If we're honest, both sides do this, in our own ways, in roughly equal proportion. Today the prevailing argument clearly has tipped in favor of the ones who claim to hold the moral high ground of featuring only popular music. It is alleged to be the only music accessible to the unsaved, and anyone who dares disagree about that must not care about evangelism. Traditionalist retort that advocates of entertainment venue music don't care about the transcendence of God. And, so, the factions scowl over the parapet at each other.

It is important, however, to establish the vast difference between what Lewis was thinking of when he referred to music of a "humbler and coarser fare" and the entertainment venue that dominates corporate worship today. The "coarser fare" has changed drastically, while the music celebrated and appreciated by those of "trained and delicate taste," by its enduring nature, remains largely as Lewis would have known it in his day.

In the six decades since Lewis's death, the "coarser fare" has managed to get far more rambunctious than

I'm sure Lewis could have ever anticipated. He died nearly a decade before the contemporary Christian music industry began to launch itself into the favored position over which it now holds almost exclusive sway.

MUSIC AND SILENCE

I do wonder what Lewis would write about today's entertainment musical fare in churches. I'm confident he would write about it; I'm equally confident it would not be overly flattering. Perhaps, what he had Screwtape declare about music and silence works as a fitting prophetic commentary on high-volume instrumental music that passes for accompaniment in entertainment worship six decades later. "Music and silence," Lewis has Screwtape bemoan, "—how I detest them both!"

> No moment of infernal time has been surrendered to either of those abominable forces, but all has been occupied by Noise—Noise, the great dynamism, the audible expression of all that is exultant, ruthless, and virile—Noise which alone defends us from silly qualms, despairing scruples, and impossible desires. We will make the whole universe a noise in the end. We have already made great strides in this direction as regards earth. The melodies and silence of Heaven will be shouted down in the end. But I admit we are not yet loud enough, or anything like it.

The manner in which Lewis makes music and silence so repugnant to the demons, who prefer loud noise over either, strongly suggests that by "music" Lewis was not referring to music of the "coarser fare," and its stepchildren in proliferating genre to the present, music that requires volume, music which seems to scream at us, "we are not yet loud enough, or anything like it."

Conversely, when God exults over his children with "loud singing," clearly the text is referring to the loudness of God's voice, and so throughout the Psalms where we are called to "break forth into joyous song and sing praises" (98:4).

In our have-technology-will-use world there are subtleties that we're no longer capable of getting, nuances that are simply lost on us. From Psalms that call for loud singing, we immediately infer that the instruments must be really loud. If loud is good, we can make it really loud. We have the technological ability to create high-octane volume with the flip of a lever. But what we're creating is high-decibel instrumental music not vocal music, singing with full voice, like God sings. We cannot have it both ways. The instrumental volume ensures that whatever vocal volume is happening far beneath it won't matter. The electronic "accompaniment" music will drown out the human voice every time.

LEWIS QUOTING HYMNS

Sprinkled here in there in what Lewis says negatively about singing and hymns, are bits and pieces of evidence that might suggest that Lewis, over time, developed an appreciation for the best of Christian hymnody.

In *Reflections on the Psalms*, he wrote, "The price of salvation is one that only the Son of God could pay; as the hymn says, 'there was no other good enough to pay the price of sin.'"

Lewis is quoting one of Irish hymn writer Cecil Frances Alexander's best-loved hymns:

There was no other good enough
To pay the price of sin;
He only could unlock the gate
Of heav'n, and let us in.

From this, I draw at least a tentative conclusion that Lewis had developed an appreciation of Alexander as a poet and hymn writer. Having been born in Belfast, Ireland himself, just three years after Alexander's death, he would likely have known other hymns she wrote.

At Christmas in the chapel of Magdalen College where he taught, Lewis would no doubt have heard the boys choir sing Alexander's grand hymn "Once in Royal David's City" to Henry Gauntlet's magisterial melody, a perennial favorite in cathedrals and churches throughout the British Isles.

Most of us don't quote poetry in a favorable light, as Lewis does in the above example, unless we appreciate it. And I strongly doubt that Lewis dismissed the best of Alexander's hymns as merely "fifth-rate poems set to sixth-rate music."

FASTS AND VIGILS

Lewis finds occasion to favorably quote another hymn in his best-selling *Screwtape Letters*. In a letter he wrote to his brother on July 21, 1940, just weeks after Warnie had been rescued off the beaches at Dunkirk,

Lewis described an idea that had come to him during the service at Holy Trinity just that morning: "Before the service was over... I was struck by an idea for a book which I think might be both useful and entertaining." And then he proceeded to outline how he would explore "the psychology of temptation from the *other* point of view" in what would become *Screwtape Letters*.

When I first learned this about how Lewis got his idea for a book on temptation in a worship service, I began wondering if the Scripture readings from the Book of Common Prayer, the sermon, and the hymns might not have all been on the theme of temptation.

And then, lo and behold, in Letter XXII, I read Screwtape's frustration about the patient being in love, and how God actually is "a hedonist at heart. All those fasts and vigils and stakes and crosses are only a façade."

Lewis was doing it again, quoting from hymn poetry. Here he was referencing the ancient hymn of St. Andrew of Crete, "Christian, Dost Thou See Them," a hymn calling Christians to awaken their various senses to the reality of how the "powers of darkness" go about tempting us, the same theme of *Screwtape*!

On my next visit to Holy Trinity, I asked the vicar Tom Honey if he thought maybe they had sung St. Andrew of Crete's hymn during that 1940 service, with the phrase "all those fasts and vigils" quoted right there on the pages of *Screwtape Letters*. Could it be that it was while singing Andrew's ancient hymn that ideas for spiritual warfare struck Lewis's imagination?

"Douglas," said the vicar, "you may very well be on to something there. That is entirely a credible possibility."

Well, we may never know the answer to that whole question, but, clearly, Lewis was quoting St. Andrew's hymn. Notice how similar in theme and tone this hymn is with *Screwtape Letters*:

Christian, dost thou see them
On the holy ground,
How the pow'rs of darkness
Rage thy steps around?
Christian, up and smite them,
Counting gain but loss,
In the strength that cometh
By the holy cross.

Each octave stanza of Andrew's hymn is organized in two quatrains to be sung as a canon, alternate parts of the congregation or the choir responding to one another: the first a call for us to see the demonic powers, to feel them, to hear them; the second part of the canon is a rousing call to action, for the Christian to "up and smite them."

Christian, dost thou feel them,
How they work within,
Striving, tempting, luring,
Goading into sin?
Christian, never tremble;
Never be downcast;
Gird thee for the battle,
Watch and pray and fast.

Christian, dost thou hear them,

How they speak thee fair?
"Always fast and vigil?
Always watch and prayer?"
Christian, answer boldly,
"While I breathe I pray!"
Peace shall follow battle,
Night shall end in day.

Without a doubt, Lewis was eluding to this stanza in *Screwtape Letters*, "Always fast and vigil." Written first in Greek, the rugged splendor of Andrew's lyric is preserved and augmented by the Victorian hymn writer John Mason Neale who rendered this poignant lyric in English in 1862. In the final stanza, Andrew with Neale's aid fittingly directs us away from the demonic powers to the words of the Savior.

Hear the words of Jesus:
"O my servant true:
Thou art very weary—
I was weary too;
But that toil shall make thee
Someday all mine own,
And the end of sorrow
Shall be near my throne."

After I had pointed out to my poetry students how Andrew appeals to various human senses in his poetry, an essential quality of all good writing, one of my witty writers, Kristianna Anderson, sensed that Andrew had missed one of the senses, so she added another stanza:

Christian dost thou smell them
With a stench so foul?
Spreading heinous odors
While they're on the prowl?
Christian do not sniff them!
By no means inhale;
Turn your nose toward heaven;
Let righteousness prevail!

Andrew's ancient hymn must have been a favorite of Lewis's friend at Oxford, the crime fiction dame, Dorothy Sayers, who wrote, "When I was a kid, did I like singing, 'We are but little children, weak'? Not on your life! I liked, 'Christian, dost thou [see] them?'—especially the bit about 'prowl and prowl around.'"

Perhaps it was frail hymns of the sentimentally anemic variety that Lewis also disliked so much.

POETRY THEN MUSIC

Six years after Neale created the English version of this ancient poem, John B. Dykes, organist and composer at Durham Cathedral, composed a two-part canonical melody for Andrew's hymn. The gritty first quatrain is sung to a sober, eerie, minor key melody, so fitting to a lyric about demons; the second quatrain response is bright and energetic, perfectly in keeping with the lyric, "Christian, answer boldly."

Here, we are reminded of the importance of the order: word and lyric coming first and guiding the musical composition. Andrew, writing in the 7th and 8th centuries, Neale and Dykes writing and composing in the 19th century, together have perfect wedded poetry and music, giving a timeless hymn for Christians to sing in every generation.

Musicians and composers would do well to study Dykes' many fine hymn tunes, beginning with Reginald Heber's "Holy, Holy, Holy," and Frances Havergal's "Take My Life, and Let It Be," Edward Perronet's "All Hail the Power of Jesus' Name," and many more. Wise composers of music to be sung in the high worship of God will shun the trend machine, what is popular and disposable, and tune their ears to what is timeless and enduring.

LEWIS SINGS NOW

In a thrilling moment in *The Magician's Nephew*, Lewis gives us a peek into the irrepressible force of music, perhaps what he truly longed for in singing. He has Aslan utter

> a long single note; not very loud, but full of power. Polly's heart jumped in her body when she heard it. She felt sure that it was a call, and that anyone who heard that call would want to obey it and (what's more) would be able to obey it, however many worlds and ages lay between.

We can be pretty certain Lewis and his brother would not be bolting from their pew and heading for the exit sign during that kind of anthem.

Though Lewis may have been overly opinionated about congregational singing in worship, and wanted "fewer, better, and shorter hymns," over time he did come to see "the great merit" of the voice of the congregation, untrained, but singing from the heart, voices joining together, making a joyful noise unto the Lord.

Three hundred years before Lewis's time, another Oxford-trained poet, Thomas Ken, wrote of glorified saints singing in heaven:

> And hymns with the supernal choir
> Incessant sing and never tire.

We're safe to assume that C. S. Lewis is doing it as we speak, singing more, the best, and longest hymns, incessant ones, right next to the man in elastic side boots who used to sing out of tune, but now who sings more like how God himself sings.

6

THE DEVIL HATES GOOSE QUILLS

Martin Luther, who said "The Devil hates goose quills," insisted that in a reformation, "We need poets." Most of us scratch our heads and wonder what on earth we need them for.

Our postmodern, post-Christian, post-Biblical culture has almost totally dismissed what used to be called poetry. Few deny it; ours is a post-poetry culture. But who cares?

POST-POETRY CULTURE

"Poetry is a marginal art form," wrote poet Campbell McGrath, "in a culture that values neither literacy nor artistic expression in any vital way. America does not persecute poets, it does not seek to smash them like bugs—it just doesn't care a lot."

Martin Luther cared deeply about poetry, in the most vital way. But do most Christians today? Most accept the decline of poetry without a whimper, with barely a wafture of good riddance. But does it matter? Paul

Johnson, decrying the decline in literacy, argues that students should "produce competent verse in a wide variety of strict meters, under examination conditions."

To what purpose should they be subjected to such literary tortures? After all, what good is it? Won't the machinations of society carry on just fine without poetry? Won't the Church do just fine without it? It's not like poetry contributes anything vital. You can't eat it.

So thought Hanoverian King George II, "I hate all boets!" he declared. If you've ever been flummoxed at lines you were told were poetry, ones about wheelbarrows and chickens, you may agree with George's abhorrence of poets.

But are Christians to stand deferentially aside as culture pitches poetry—the highest form—into the lowest circle of hell?

WHAT HAPPENED TO POETRY?

I've been accused of the pedagogical unpardonable sin of depriving my writing students of what has become poetry's sole consideration: individual self-expression. "Why don't you let them write in free verse?" I'm asked. "I do," I reply. "We just call it brainstorming."

Arguably *vers libre* achieved its foothold with Walt Whitman, a man with new ideas simmering in his bosom, new ideas that demanded a new form. "Through me forbidden voices, voices of sexes and lust, voices veiled, and I removed the veil." The Devil, no doubt, rubs his hands in glee at Whitman's goose quill.

Whitman-like free verse dictates against any conventional structure of meter or rhyme. This throw-off-the-shackles impulse creates a blurring of literary genre wherein poetic form is abandoned in favor of irregular bursts of feeling. What often remains is merely fragmented prose. "Poetry" thus conceived provides a pseudo-form for saying private things about one's self, things one would never utter in direct speech—until Whitman removed the veil.

Such redefining of what poetry is has led to a proliferation of what one classics professor termed, "therapeutic soul-baring by emotional exhibitionist[s]." Or as John Stott quipped, "The trouble with you Americans is you're constantly engaged in a spiritual strip-tease."

Abandoning form for raw emotion is not unique to poets. Most artists are quite pleased with themselves for smashing outmoded forms in favor of new structures, ones better suited to self-expression, the now primary sphere of art.

It's no coincidence that poetry began its descent into "gaseous emotionalizing" in egalitarian America. Alexis de Tocqueville placed the blame squarely on the devolutions of democracy. "Nothing is more repugnant to the human mind, in an age of equality, than the idea of subjection to forms."

As he continues, one wonders if de Tocqueville was thinking of his contemporary Walt Whitman. "Democracy diverts the imagination from all that is external to man, and fixes it on man alone. Each citizen is habitually engaged in the contemplation of a very puny object, namely, himself."

Meanwhile, Whitman was working on his signature poem, "Song of Myself," the prototype of vacuous praise—of the wrong object. Man-centered praise poetry was born. Instead of "turning us from ourselves to [God]" as Whitman's contemporary, John Greenleaf Whittier wrote, "Song of Myself" set the mortar of poetic self-referentialism.

Much of Whitman's poetry was disgusting material. "I believe in the flesh and the appetites," he crooned.

> Divine am I inside and out…
> The scent of these armpits aroma finer than prayer,
> This head more than churches, bibles, and all the
> creeds… nothing, not God, is greater… more
> wonderful than myself.

One wishes Whitman would stop. But he does not. Nor have poets since.

When Whittier received his advance copy of "Song of Myself," he read a few lines and tossed it into the fire. Unfortunately, *vers libre* emotive self-expression survived the burning. One tragic result is that we've forfeited the ability to measure the quality of poetry, so free verse proliferates without censure as everyone and his cocker spaniel gets in touch with the poet within.

POETRY IN THE BIBLE

The Devil likely applauds Christians who shrug indifferently as genuine poetry spirals into the abyss. Yet the Bible contains the finest poetry of the ancient world. Hebrew poetry, divinely inspired, not only adorned the highest object, it was the greatest lyric beauty ever penned, C. S. Lewis considering Psalm 19 the finest poem of all time.

All people in the ancient world turned to poetry. It is the *imago Dei* in human beings that they express their deepest longings, their highest joys, and their darkest grief in poetry. Contrary to today's post-poetry world, if we had lived 3,000 years ago in the ancient near-east under the blessing of the Sovereign Lord, poetry would have played a daily role in our lives. We would have sung it, danced to it, memorized it, prayed it, written it, accompanied it on our lyre, hummed it as we herded sheep, shouted it charging into battle, and lifted our voice with inspired poetry in corporate worship with the grand assembly of Israel, the accelerating wonder of the presence of the Almighty thrilling our souls. At last, we would have parted this life with Psalms on our lips in our final sigh.

Throughout every season of our existence, our lives would have revolved around grand poetic expressions of adoration, ones such as my father's favorite (Psalm 34) as he was dying of cancer:

This poor man cried, and the LORD heard him
and saved him out of all his troubles.
The angel of the LORD encamps
around those who fear him, and he delivers them.
Oh, taste and see that the LORD is good!
Blessed is the man who takes refuge in him!

Line upon line, Psalms are full of passionate expressions of hope and adoration, rich, exuberant poetry that appears throughout the historical and prophetic books as well.

The Apostle Paul, Hebrew of the Hebrews, not only knew the Psalms, he understood pagan verse. Speaking before the Areopagus (Acts 17:28), he recited from pagan Greek poet, Epimenides of Crete, "In him we live and move and have our being," and from Aratus's Phainomena, with the line, "For we are indeed his offspring." And Daniel was "competent to stand in the king's palace" for his wisdom and to have it augmented by being taught "the literature and language of the Chaldeans" (Daniel 1:4), literature which in the ancient world would have been exclusively poetry.

POETRY IN GENEVA

While Luther searched for German poets, psalms versified for singing became central to the progress of the gospel in the French Reformation. Calvin employed the fugitive court poet, Clement Marot, to create French psalm versifications for the *Geneva Psalter* (1551). Calvin himself may have inked his goose quill to craft the psalm-like hymn "I Greet Thee Who My sure Redeemer Art." Though not a strict versification of any psalm text, it was included in the Psalter.

So central was psalm singing to the Reformation that by Calvin's death there were sixty illegal French psalters in circulation throughout Europe. Without a doubt, some of these versifications were of considerably better poetic quality than others. However faithful to the original Psalm in theology, and however sincere the poet, many of these versifications were poetically crude material.

Nevertheless, biblical Christians will always want to sing psalms, and there are fine existing psalm versifications to sing. But ought we to keep singing the ones that contort syntax to fit the meter, the ones that are clearly not words set in delightful proportion, as the inspired Psalms so clearly were?

Poet physician, Elliot Emanuel, observed that "poetry is what eludes translation." Though original truths can be translated, the subtle nuances of poetic language are another matter. Unique cadences and conventions inevitably must give way to those of the new language. Though raw content remains, the words in the new language rarely can convey the soul of the poetry.

Poetry's role is to adorn truth by creating pictures with words, figurative language; and by creating music with words, employing sound devices like alliteration, rhyming, and enjambment. Though parallelisms of idea translate from Hebrew to other languages, the mysterious and wonderful images and music created with words in the original poetry are often lost. Hence, when faithful men labored to make strict, metered English verse from Hebrew Psalm poetry, complications arose. To their credit, these men intentionally paid much greater attention to the inspired content than to the lyric devices of English poetry. But must it be either or?

POETRY THE DEVIL HATES

Though there are enduring versifications in English psalters, we've all stumbled along attempting to sing some versions. Let's be honest. There are psalm versifications that are clumsy poetry. I hasten to add that this is no criticism of psalm singing—and certainly not of the inspired text. Nothing could be further from my intention. It's simply candor.

Consider an illustration. Determined to worship God biblically, the Massachusetts Bay Colony employed linguist and missionary John Elliot to versify Psalms directly from the Hebrew original. The resulting *Bay Psalm Book* (1640) was the first book published in the New World, a monument to the priority of psalm singing in Christian worship. But clearly poetic beauty in English was not a prominent objective:

> O Blessed man, that in th'advice
> of wicked men doeth not walk:
> Or stand in sinners' way, or sit
> in chair of scornful folk.

Though the original Psalm is divinely inspired poetry, the *Bay Psalm Book* version of Psalm 1 is indisputably not an example of "words set in delightful proportion," as Sir Philip Sidney defined poetry in his classic work *Defense of Poesy*.

Herein is the great dilemma for educators: We rightly train our students to appreciate the grandeur of the canon of English poetry, words and meaning set in delightful proportion by John Donne and others, while we require them to sing sometimes awkward English poetry back to God in corporate worship. Like teaching them to craft fine wine but making them drink purple Kool Aid.

Certainly, the Devil hates it when we get the theological content correct. But I'd wager he's content when we leave poetry to musty bookshelves. I suspect he beams with delight when a generation attempts to worship the God who made a universe of stupendous beauty with halting poetic efforts.

Meanwhile, the Psalms call us to gaze upon the beauty of the Lord, to be dazzled at his loveliness—and they do so with inspired poetry, the finest ever penned, adorning glorious truths about God's perfections and redemptive ways, set in the most surpassingly delightful proportion.

Just as the musicians chosen to accompany psalm singing in old covenant worship were to be men of unrivalled musical skill, so much more in new covenant worship, the content and the form of the poetry ought to be the finest. Imagine the diabolical hand-wringing when it is so.

CHRISTOLOGIC PREACHING AND SINGING

We would rightly consider a preacher of the gospel to have missed the point if he preached through a book of the law and concluded that finally what matters is our obedience, as if Paul never wrote that the law was a schoolmaster to lead us to Christ, our righteousness, the fulfillment of the law.

Moreover, if he preached from an old covenant poetic book but taught it as nothing more than ancient, near-eastern love poetry, devoid of redemptive typology, devoid of Christ the lover of his bride the Church, we would rightly feel that Christ had been dishonored in such preaching—and we had been cheated.

Redemptive-historical preaching is not a hermeneutical option, a matter of methodological taste that works for some and not for others. In his book

Christ-Centered Preaching, Brian Chappell wrote, "The redemptive-historical method… is a vital and foundational tool that expositors need to accurately and gracefully interpret texts in their full context." No other method gets at the burden of the biblical text—Jesus. So when Paul writes that we are "in word or deed" to do all in the name of the Lord Jesus, in the immediate context of singing "psalms, hymns, and spiritual songs" (Colossians 3:16-17), perhaps we ought to consider that what is true of preaching in new covenant worship is equally true of singing in new covenant worship.

"The hymns of Luther," a Jesuit critic said, "killed more souls than his sermons." Preacher Isaac Watts is not remembered for his sermons; like Luther, poet Watts is remembered for his hymns. One reason is that he vigorously combined his redemptive-historical interpretation with vital poetry adorning the highest object.

Watts' versification of Psalm 72 provides a concise example. "Give the king your justice, O God," fashioned by Watts' redemptive-historical theology and his poetic skill, became, "Jesus shall reign where e'er the sun / Doth his successive journeys run." Poets like Luther and Watts, who used their goose quills to adorn the loveliness of Jesus—the Devil abhors. Let's give him more to hate.

LET'S SHARPEN THOSE GOOSE QUILLS

"We need poets," said Luther, as does the Church today, poets laboring to master that mysterious human expression that flows directly from our being God's image bearers. Excellence in poetry is supremely a gift of

God, but honing poetic skill requires study, imitation, submission to form, practice, and experience, just like playing the cello or the banjo.

Poetry, as with all gifts of God, ought to be used for its highest purpose. "The highest form of poetry is the hymn," wrote Whittier, arch-critic of Whitman, whose object was himself. If poetry adorns and delineates the ideal, what possible higher ideal could there be—than Christ himself?

Even French Catholic de Tocqueville felt uneasy about American poets using their quills to gush about streams and mountains—and themselves—instead of celebrating "the providential designs that rule the universe, [that] show the finger of the Supreme Governor, [that] reveal the thoughts of the Supreme Mind," notably themes appearing in Psalms and the finest hymn poetry.

I wonder how many of us have thought of the words we were singing in worship as the highest form of poetry. There may be reasons for this. It may be because much of it is "gaseous emotionalism" with vague Bible words—so unlike inspired Psalm poetry. Or, though the words may be true, it may simply be mediocre poetry, uninspiring, pedestrian verse.

We may be tempted to assume that we already have good enough hymns—and there are many fine ones—so how important can it be to produce poets and new hymns? Maybe Luther got it wrong. I suspect the Devil nods approvingly at this reasoning.

But aren't there plenty of great sermons? Why not simply read from the vast wealth of existing sermons preached by able expositors like Luther, Calvin,

Edwards, and Spurgeon? Yet Christians understand that every healthy age in the Church will produce preachers—skillful men who preach God's Word afresh and with Spirit-imbued power.

Without straining the comparison, won't every age want to frustrate the Devil by producing poets who honor Christ anew in their poetry? The Devil hates goose quills, including ones wielded by able poets who train their pens to the highest use—crafting psalm-like hymns that lift the heart, mind, and imagination from our puny selves, and enthrall us with Christ alone.

The Devil probably enjoys what Whitman and his offspring spew, but he hates real poetry. Judging from the vast quantity of poetry in the inspired canon of the Bible—God loves poetry. And so must his bride, the Church.

Imagine the Devil's despair when Christians train their children to know and love God's Word and render to their Redeemer the most stupendous words of gratitude and adoration—highest register words, worthy of the highest object. Let's sharpen those goose quills and discover the Cowper and Rossetti lying dormant in this generation.

7

MISSING REASONS

If you're at all like I am, you've heard things being sung in worship that sounded far more like we were all merely singing about what we were singing about. "I just want to praise the Lord," always made me wonder why he didn't just do it then, rather than sing repeatedly, over and over again, that that's what he just wants to do.

I'VE GOT A REASON

We attended what was called a fine arts concert at a Christian school some time ago, and it jolted me into considering how different our singing is from how God reveals in his Word that he and his people will sing.

One of the pieces they sang was entitled "I've Got a Reason." It was a model of singing about what we're singing about. I am not exaggerating to say that the title of the song is half of the lyric to the whole song: "I've got a reason to praise the Lord." As near as I could hear the words, that was it, sung over and over and over again, with nothing said about what that reason was. This was not a 7-11 song, seven words sung eleven times over. It was a 7-70 song, seven words sung seventy times, though I entirely lost count. The music was loud, sassy, and I assume appealing to the particular audience for which it was concocted.

At one point in the concert, the gentleman emceeing the event stepped onto the stage, fog machine doing its work, floodlights oscillating throughout the "experience center," as they called their gathering place; he stepped onto the stage and said, "Here, we don't put on a concert. We put on a show," which he hastened to equate with a worship experience.

There was a good deal of talk about being a Jesus person, that it was all about the gospel. But did I miss it? The name of Jesus, I do not believe, was ever uttered in any of the lyrics sung. Mind you, the instruments were loud, the performers' voices were raucous and inarticulate, the words virtually incomprehensible.

For all the talk about Jesus at intervals between songs (intervals for fund raising), why would we not hear his name at least mentioned all evening in any of the lyrics? And the closest thing to the gospel I heard was the vague theme of changing one's identity, largely by self-help and emotional resolve, but there was never clarity about what causes the change. What was clear, was that once changed, people will accept who they are and stop trying to fit in the boxes others have made for them.

Afterward in the car on the way home, my daughter rather uncharitably remarked, "Someone needs to give these people a dictionary." She went on to reveal that her friends in the choir admitted that, simplistic as the lyrics were, they didn't really know the words, but then that didn't really matter; they were there to back up the soloist with vocal sounds: "When they don't know the words, they just repeat 'I've Got a Reason' and keep dancing and swaying."

While many may recognize that "I've Got a Reason to Praise the Lord," is not saying very much at all, and certainly is guilty of the glaring omission of never actually getting around to saying what the reason is, we might be inclined to dismiss it as an anomaly. Surely, there has to be a contemporary lyric that is far better, that gives at least some reasons for the praise.

MUSIC FIRST

We can rejoice that there is. Anything written by Stuart Townend and the Gettys is in an altogether higher lyrical and theological category from the above example. As well-loved as "In Christ Alone" has become, however, Matt Redman's "10,000 Reasons" far exceeds it as one of the all-time contemporary favorites, for a long period of time being the number one most sung worship song in American churches.

Highly acclaimed immediately after its release in 2012, "10,000 Reasons" shot to the top spot on Christian Radio and remained there for sixteen weeks; it also was No. 1 on the *Billboard* Christian Songs Chart for thirteen weeks and achieved a gold certification. In 2013, the song won two Grammy Awards for both Best Contemporary Christian Music Song and Best Gospel/Contemporary Christian Music Performance categories. Additionally, the song won the 2013 Gospel Music Association's "Dove Award for Song of the Year." The lyricist who penned the words also won the "Contemporary Christian performance of the year" for his performance of his song at the 44th GMA Dove Awards event.

Though Redman gets the credit for the popularity of this song, Jonas Myrin who came up with the tune before there ever was a lyric, deserves far more of the credit. It is an accelerating tune that gets inside your head. Whatever your predisposition about contemporary musical styles, you will have a hard time not singing this tune in the shower. It begins with two anticipatory beats that draw you into the emotive aura of the melody.

Redman told *Worship Leader* magazine how it all happened. "[Jonas Myrin] played me an idea for some of the chorus melody, and I found it immediately inspiring. In fact, it felt like a perfect fit for a song based on the opening of Psalm 103. The song came together really quickly—a good chunk of the song was actually a spontaneous moment."

As interesting as it is to hear how a song came about, does anybody think that David first came up with a really cool riff on his harp and then cast about for some good lyrics to go with it? And out popped "a good chunk" of Psalm 103 in "a spontaneous moment"? Redman's reversal of the biblical priority of the word, his lyrics appearing almost as an afterthought to the tune, has become the common occurrence in contemporary Christian music making.

Lest we think this is merely a contemporary problem, being moved more by the music than by the substance of the lyric was a problem Calvin needed to caution his congregation about in Geneva. Calvin and court poet Clement Marot first spent many months versifying the psalms into metrical poetry; only afterward did they present the words to Louis Bourgeois for him to create appropriate music for congregational singing of those words. If Calvin's warning was relevant five centuries ago in Geneva, how much more so must we beware of making music more important than the content of what we are singing?

To speak bluntly, people sing "10,000 Reasons" not because the words are beautifully arranged and so deep and moving. Without Myrin's tune, this metrically irregular lyric, tacked on after the fact, on its own merits, as lines of poetry, would not amount to much.

One of the best ways to evaluate the worth of any new lyric is to set the music aside and read it as poetry, and then measure it alongside the finest poetry. All the best hymns began first as poetry written to long-standing conventions, based on the writer's study, understanding, and appreciation of the finest poetry in the language. We shouldn't bother singing anything to God that does not measure up, in its own right, to the high standard of the finest, the truest, the most beautiful poetry. After all, that's what David did.

When Redman heard Myrin's tune, his mind moved in a good direction; he thought of what David wrote in the opening lines of Psalm 103, "Bless the Lord, O my soul." After repeating "O my soul,"

Redman then calls the singer to "worship his holy name." So far so good. But then, while the psalmist enlists "all that is within me" to the glorious task of blessing the holy name of the Lord, apparently Redman wasn't sure what to do with that phrase, so he calls us to "Sing like never before."

LIKE NEVER BEFORE

What, pray tell, does this phrase actually mean? Sing better than we sang it last week, or the week before? As many times as this song has been sung over and again millions of times, this phrase creates a nonsensical standard, a ceiling that keeps getting higher with each repetition. Presumably, there is a limitation to singing it like never before. David's "all that is within me" is far better because it is true and repeatable; I can call my soul next week to bless the Lord with "all that is within me," though it is bewilderingly meaningless to call my soul to "Sing like never before."

This kind of sentimental dishonesty reminds me of congregations in past generations rising with all their neighbors and lustily singing "and the joy we share, as we tarry there, none other has ever known." Wait, so all the other people in the congregation are singing that each of them individually shares a joy with the Lord that "none other has ever known"? Not only is it poetry of the cheap-perfume variety, it's individualistic ooze. The very act of singing it requires flagrant insulting of the devotion of the people singing it all around me, who don't share the joy I am sharing with the Lord, alone there in the garden, known only by me.

More problematic still, Redman has us singing "like never before" at least six times over in the same song, presumably each time requires a higher standard than the time we sang it before even within the song itself, that's assuming the worship leader doesn't feel the Spirit move him to repeat the chorus a few more times—each time, presumably, like never before.

FORGET NOT

David doesn't do that to us. While Redman reduces "all that is within me" to the emotionally unattainable, David calls his soul and ours to "forget not all his benefits," and then proceeds to enumerate, line-upon-line, reason-upon-reason, all those benefits. David knows we are forgetful people. He knows we will forget that it is the "Lord who works righteousness and justice for all who are oppressed." Or we will forget that "God does not deal with us according to our sins, nor repay us according to our iniquities." So often in contemporary lyrics sin is reduced or ignored altogether. What good is it to our souls if God is "rich in love" if we don't first understand "that we are dust," that our "days are like grass"?

Notice in David's magisterial lyric the extensive use of figurative language, evocative images created with words that the Holy Spirit must believe our souls need in order to grasp these marvelous truths. We need the imaginative comparison of being satisfied with the goodness of God "so that [our] youth is renewed like the eagle's." The psalmists are

110

constantly drawing pictures for us, awakening our imagination, renewing our minds: "...as high as the heavens are above the earth, so great is his steadfast love toward those who fear him." The fear of God is a theme seldom if ever explored by the contemporary lyricist matching his words to a catchy tune his friend plucked out on the guitar. The lyrics have to fit that tune, or it just won't fly, won't get the acclaim, the plays on radio stations, the awards. It has to fit the latest popular musical sound. At the end of the day, it's the catchy tune that carries the day.

David no doubt plucked the strings of his harp to Psalm 103, but the melody was subservient to the lyric, enhancing and undergirding the words. Since we are to "forget not all his benefits," the psalmist bends every imaginative nerve to enumerate those benefits, or, put another way, to enumerate the 10,000 reasons and more we have to "Bless the Lord, O my soul."

TIME TO SING—AGAIN

We must tune our literary ears before we presume to set pen to paper and write what we hope the Church will sing in the high worship of God. The best way to do that is to saturate our minds and hearts in the Bible, especially in Psalms. "It's time to sing your song again," the opening line of the first stanza of Redman's song, when held up next to Psalm 103, is a somewhat anemic expression. It could easily be, ho hum; it's morning and I have to get up and sing your song—*again*. While this emotionally appealing song is made up of three stanzas of singing about keeping on singing, there's nothing lyrically inventive, there's little to awaken the heart, little to renew the mind, and little to open wide the eyes of faith. One needs to return to David's lyric in Psalm 103 for that.

Or one will need to turn to poet hymn writers who had bathed their minds, hearts, and imaginations in Psalms, a number of whom wrote with skill and devotion about Christians singing. One fine example is Samuel Crossman who demonstrates that we do not have to forfeit passion and deep feeling when our songs are lyrically and theologically attuned:

> My song is love unknown,
> My Saviors love to me,
> Love to the loveless shown
> That they might lovely be.
> O, who am I
> That for my sake
> My Lord should take
> Frail flesh and die?

While the central connecting idea of Redman's song is three stanzas about our determination to keep on singing—whatever, Crossman's song runs to the Savior, points away from my singing, and in subsequent stanzas, to a rich and layered series of passionately expressed reasons for singing, concluding:

> Here might I stay and sing,
> No story so divine;
> Never was love, dear King,
> Never was grief like thine.

This is my Friend,
In whose sweet praise
I all my days
Could gladly spend.

If we are to sing about singing, surely this is more the way a worshipful Christian will want to do so.

WHATEVER MAY PASS

David in Psalm 103 thrills us with the sovereignty of God in all of our affairs when he calls our souls to consider that God our compassionate father, "established his throne in the heavens, and his kingdom rules over all." But in "10,000 Reasons" this truth is almost entirely absent; we're left with the anemic phrase "Whatever may pass and whatever lies before me." This inadequate expression falls short because it simply cannot bear the weight of its topic. We're not given any reason why we should keep on singing whatever happens; apparently, singing is just therapeutic and its own cure, like whistling in the dark. The high sovereignty of God ruling tenderly over all of my life requires far higher register language, language like the psalmist uses and the great hymn writers after him.

Observe the stark contrast between Redman's diminutive phrase and how Welsh poet Anna Waring develops the same theme of God's providential guiding and governing of whatever happens in our lives:

Father, I know that all my life
Is portioned out for me.
The changes that are sure to come,

I do not fear to see.
I ask thee for a present mind
Intent on pleasing thee.

A FEW REASONS

While we too easily take a theologically reductionist path and bow to commercial interests in our singing, David is just getting warmed up. "[A]s far as the east is from the west, so far does he remove our transgressions from us." The psalmist can't stop, and he marshals more figurative language to awaken the eyes of faith.

In the second stanza, Redman seems to realize, given the title of his song, he had better get at least a few reasons on the table. Unlike many songs in this genre, to his credit, the lyricist does give us reasons— a few of them. Nothing like 10,000, however. Far from it. So very unlike the whole of the Psalms, all we are given is a fairly short list of several attributes of God: his love, his slowness to anger, his greatness, his kindness, his goodness.

This is good, as far as it goes. But held next to Psalm 103, it falls far short. Unlike David's lyric, there is little or no elaboration or illustration of those attributes. Wanting us to "forget not all his benefits," the psalmist takes nearly ten verses to describe our sin and unworthiness and "the steadfast love of the Lord [which] is from everlasting to everlasting" on sinners and "his righteousness to children's children." All of which content is entirely absent in the Redman song.

DEATH

One of the themes reoccurring in psalms, hymns, and so fervently in African-American Spirituals but that is almost entirely absent in the praise songs, worship songs, and choruses of the last generation—is death. Redman attempts to do what many of his contemporaries were neglecting: have something about death in his song. Written by zealous musicians, many of them new Christians, young and inexperienced in the faith and in life, illness and death were not themes that seemed overly important to many song writers in the last few decades.

To his credit Redman makes an effort at fixing this in his final stanza:

And on that day when my strength is failing,
The end draws near and my time has come.

And then he resumes his central idea of continuing to sing, in this last stanza, forevermore. Yet, significantly absent is any clear articulation of the reasons his soul continues to sing God's praises unendingly, particularly ironic considering the song's title. At its worst, this is a song that celebrates self-redemption by my determination to keep on singing, like never before.

But how different from Psalms. Redman can only bring himself to use a modern cliché for death, "my time has come," a euphemism that springs from the secular notion that death is just a natural part of life, but not so David.

The psalmist summons all his poetic skill. He wants us to feel the full weight of the reality of death, but also of the wonder of God's steadfast love that alone rescues us from death:

> For he knows our frame;
> he remembers that we are dust.
> As for man, his days are like grass;
> he flourishes like a flower of the field;
> for the wind passes over it, and it is gone,
> and its place knows it no more (14-16).

Redman concludes his song by returning to our singing like never before. But David does something very different. He is overwhelmed, beside himself at the splendor of who God is and what he has savingly accomplished for his children: The God of mercy and grace, who removes our sins from us, who is steadfast in love for his children; the Lord who "works righteousness" for his own. The psalmist gives expansively enumerated reasons to bless the Lord for the glory of his saving work on behalf of sinners. So overwhelmed by those reasons, David seems to feel that his own soul is inadequate to bless such a saving God as this. So, he concludes in a majestic finale wherein he calls on angels, the mighty ones, the heavenly hosts, God's ministers, all dominions, all God's works to join him and "Bless the Lord."

ANGELS, HELP US TO ADORE HIM

Though there are myriad examples throughout the canon of Christian hymnody, the contrast between Redman's and Henry Lyte's lyric, "Praise My Soul, the King of Heaven," both inspired by Psalm 103, may be the most important illustration of the shift from literary and theological substance to the literarily bland and the theologically reductionist.

To my knowledge, Lyte's hymn never won any awards, or made it to the number one spot on any chart or radio rankings. Nevertheless, 200 years later, paired with John Goss's 1868 tune, Christians who truly want to bless the Lord in song, cannot stop singing Lyte's hymn. One reviewer called this hymn "certainly one of the most satisfying for congregations" to sing. Notice the rich and varied allusions to David's language in the Psalm, for example: "The Lord has established his throne in the heavens, and his kingdom rules over all" (103:19).

> Praise, my soul, the King of Heaven,
> To his feet thy tribute bring;
> Ransomed, healed, restored, forgiven,
> Who like thee his praise should sing?
> Praise him! Praise him!
> Praise him! Praise him!
> Praise the everlasting King!
>
> Praise him for his grace and favor
> To our fathers in distress;
> Praise him, still the same forever,
> Slow to chide, and swift to bless;

Here, Lyte appeals to redemptive history, God's covenant faithfulness, the substantive reasons behind God being slow to wrath and rich in love. The poet ends every stanza with a twofold "Praise him!" followed by an echo of the same, then a final varied line, in this stanza, "Glorious in His faithfulness."

In the third stanza, Lyte captures the spirit of Psalm 103 and its emphasis on God as covenant-keeping father of his children and theirs.

> Father-like, he tends and spares us;
> Well our feeble frame he knows;
> In his hands he gently bears us,
> Rescues us from all our foes;
> Praise him! Praise him!
> Praise him! Praise him!
> Widely as his mercy flows.

Unlike many modern worship songs, but so very like the psalmists, Lyte and the best hymn writers never shy away from the biblical emphasis on death. Here, Lyte uses beautiful language to celebrate the Psalm's imagery, then contrasts our mortality with the unchanging eternality of God and his promises to his own.

> Frail as summer's flower we flourish,
> Blows the wind and it is gone;
> But while mortals rise and perish,
> God endures unchanging on...
> Praise the High Eternal One!

In keeping with David's plea to angels and all God's works to join his soul in blessing the Lord, Lyte's appeal to the angels thrills our hearts, and compels our voices to join the panoply of the cosmos in praising this most worthy "God of grace."

Angels, help us to adore him;
Ye behold him face to face!
Sun and moon, bow down before him,
Dwellers all in time and space,
Praise him! Praise him!
Praise him! Praise him!
Praise with us the God of grace!

It is no overstatement to say that Lyte's poetic paraphrase of Psalm 103 resides in another literary and theological stratosphere from Redman's lyrical afterthought. Even if Myrin's catchy tune helps us sing, what are we left singing? Very little of the substance of Psalm 103 remains intact. Most notably absent are the many expansively explored reasons for blessing the Lord. Whereas Redman's words turn us back on ourselves and leave us largely singing about our determination to keep singing, Lyte, on the other hand, captures the theological richness of the Psalm: "Ransomed, healed, restored, forgiven,/Who like thee his praise should sing?"

Some are quick to object. Redmon's lyric is more accessible, and Myrin's tune is more fun to sing. Critics claim that Lyte's poetry is simply too complex for the modern worshiper. It's too theologically dense. It requires too much of us.

All that is true, a matter of fact. But then, isn't that exactly why the psalmist calls his soul "and all that is within [him]" to bless the Lord? God's ways are, indeed,

119

high above our understanding, our ability to grasp; higher than the heavens are above the earth, in fact (Isaiah 55:8-9). David illustrates this by his final appeal to angels and the entire cosmos to help us in this grand privilege of worship.

Worship is going to stretch us beyond anything that comes readily to hand. Though we were made for worshiping the living God, broken and distorted beyond recognition by the Fall, true worship—worship in spirit and in truth—is going to require the transformative, almighty power of God. True worship has never been about what we are capable of doing. It's always been about what God alone by his sovereign omnipotence has done in us, "rescu[ing] us from all our foes."

WHICH WOULD GOD SING?

What and how would the angels David and Lyte call to join them, how would they sing? How and what would God sing? We know the answer. God has revealed it to us in his Word. Certainly, God and the angels, the entire cosmos, including us, would sing Psalm 103—the uncut, unabridged version—the one God by his Holy Spirit inspired David to pen. Surely, we can all agree about that.

And as we sing "new songs" to the Lord, as we are called to do throughout the Psalms, in Isaiah, in Revelation, which of these "new songs" is most in keeping with the songs God inspired in his Word? Henry Lyte's version or Redman and Myrin's version? Which poetry lifts us most beyond ourselves? Which one most biblically celebrates the attributes of God, his fatherly way with his children, his eternal redemptive purposes? Which one thrills us, not first with the music, but thrills our hearts—and all that is within us—with God himself?

8

PLAYING AT WORSHIP

One pundit quipped that Americans "worship their work, work at their play, and play at their worship." I suspect that most Christians would object. Entertainment evangelism "worship," for them, is the best thing that's happened to church; the building is full, and look how happy everybody is.

But the numbers may be skewed. According to a 2019 Pew Research Center study, in a single decade young people identifying as Christian plunged by 16%. How we can continue to maintain that the entertainment ethos grows churches while fewer and fewer people claim to be Christians, is beyond me. Similarly, a study conducted by the Barna Research Group concluded that, though five out of six males consider themselves on some level to be Christians, only two out of six regularly go to church. They may be full, but many American churches are two thirds female and one third male.

There are many reasons for this, but changes in music may take center stage. But the debate over worship music, ironically, isn't very much about worship. Few proponents of entertainment worship music ask what music is appropriate for the worship of God. Instead, with the best of intentions, "They imitate the nations around them" (II Kings 16:10; 17:15-41) in an effort to make the gospel seem more relevant to unbelievers' tastes and, thereby, evangelize them.

A leading church-growth expert candidly admits this. "What kind of music do you listen to?" he asked the folks in his community. "I didn't have one person who said, 'I listen to organ music.' Not one. It was 96-97% adult contemporary, middle-of-the-road pop. So, we made a strategic decision that we are unapologetically a contemporary-music church."

Well-intentioned Christians have reinvented what goes on at church by shifting the question. Young church planters generally ask: "What does the world like to listen to?" rather than "What music is appropriate to worship God in the splendor of his holiness" (I Chronicles 16: 29b-30a)? Thus, church growth becomes the all-excusing rationale for what people sing in church. And they tell us it's working. One church-growth expert credited his shift to entertainment worship with why his church "exploded with growth."

No doubt attendance did increase. As it did for Roman emperors who packed out arenas by giving entertainment-crazed citizens what they liked. People showed up in droves. We too are a culture that values amusement. We like to feel good. We like to sway and clap. We like celebrity. And we'll pay for it. Church-growth proponents argue that cashing in on the postmodern infatuation with entertaining music is essential to evangelism and will fill churches.

Cultural analyst Neil Postman, a secular Jew, speculated at what price it would fill them: "Christianity is a demanding and serious religion," he wrote. "When it is delivered as easy and amusing, it is another kind of religion altogether." Postman readily acknowledged "that religion can be made entertaining. The question is, by doing so, do we destroy it." So observed a secularist looking on as he watched Christianity "shuffle off to Bethlehem," as he termed it.

When churches fashion worship to entertain the world, to give people what they want, it sets us up for constant revision and change. Though zealous church leaders use the pragmatic argument—it works and is filling churches—and their intentions may truly be to evangelize, recasting Christianity to fit the culture will inevitably alter the message. Ever-changing cultural values will demand it. To keep up, churches will find themselves taking away a little of this, adding a little of that, eventually watering down the gospel. Making Christian worship appealing to a radically changing culture will make the message less offensive—and, thereby, less Christian.

Whenever Israel imitated the pagan worship of the nations around them, God became angry and judged them. Thus, John Calvin urged that "all human inventions in worship be removed and driven from us, which God himself justly abominates." Far from aping the world, Christians ought to stand against the impulse to reinvent worship so it looks and sounds like the world.

MORE VOLUME

In *Screwtape Letters*, C. S. Lewis described heaven as a region of music and silence. Senior demon Screwtape is frustrated by this reality: "Music and silence—how I detest them both!" He boasts that in hell: "The melodies and silence of Heaven will be shouted down in the end. But I admit we are not yet loud enough, or anything like it."

Advocates of shaping worship to fit the entertainment ethos seem to ignore or dismiss the point Lewis was getting at. "We are loud," said one mega-church pastor. "We are really, really loud. I say, 'We're not gonna turn it down.'"

But does high-volume rock and roll fit with the music and silence that Lewis describes, or does it sound more like the noise and loudness Screwtape and many church growth leaders prefer? Perhaps this isn't as hard a question as we've made it.

Nevertheless, it would appear that most church musicians agree with pop music expert Don Butler, "Every style and form of music can become gospel, whether it's jazz, pop, rock and roll, or rap." The current wisdom insists that there's no particular kind of music that is more appropriate than any other for corporate worship. Anything will do. Music is neutral, and any style can be used for good ends in church.

But there is that nagging episode in *Lord of the Rings* where Boromir attempts a similar line of reasoning. Rather than destroy the ring, he urged the fellowship to use the power of the ring—for good ends. Like many in the Church, Boromir, too, was certain that he would not be corrupted by it. Tolkien seemed to think he was wrong about that.

If music is neutral, and any style can be used to convey any message, then why don't dentists play the Ring Wraith music from the Lord of the Rings soundtrack as you sit in the waiting room before your root canal? Because dentists know music is not neutral.

Beware. If entertainment-evangelism advocates can convince you that music is amoral, merely a matter of taste, then the discussion ends—and so does discernment. Students of logic will be suspicious of conclusions that conveniently sweep away moral judgment and deeper consideration.

MORAL OR AMORAL

In the preface to the *Geneva Psalter* of 1545, Calvin wrote of music that "there is hardly anything in the world with more power to turn the morals of men." Yet Christians today insist that "Music is amoral." As if to say, "Just use the ring!"

But historically nobody has thought music was amoral. Agnostic Ralph Vaughan Williams in his Preface to The English Hymnal wrote, "Good music for worship is a moral issue. The eternal gospel cannot be commended with disposable, fashionable music styles, otherwise there is the implication that the gospel itself is somehow disposable and temporary." Tragically, well-intentioned Christians, drawn in by the amoral argument, may be undermining the gospel by making it appear throwaway to the watching world.

Paste in whatever words you want, loud entertainment music already conveys its own message.

Certainly, it makes people clap and feel exhilarated, but it's not conducive to careful thinking about the whole counsel of God. Entertainment music creates a feel-good atmosphere, but it doesn't work well to make us feel bad. It more easily trivializes and vulgarizes than ennobles. It does excitement and infatuation well but is largely bankrupt on conviction and repentance— essentials not only of biblical evangelism but of sanctification, growth in grace, and true worship in spirit and in truth.

Traditionally, music in church was employed to commend the objective message, to play second fiddle to the words. But entertainment evangelism switches this around. Eager to "imitate the nations around them," musicians force the high objective truths of the Bible into the background. Thus, worship songs repeatedly state adoration but with few if any doctrinal reasons given to biblically support and adorn those statements. And increasingly the object of adoration is vague.

Gene Edward Veith, writing for *World Magazine,* concluded his review of a wide range of popular Christian materials: "So much of this Christian material says nothing about Jesus Christ."

How ironic! I thought evangelism was the reason for using entertainment music. How effective can music evangelism be if we remove the explicit Christian content from the lyrics? Though the Bible is clear, Christ is "a stone of stumbling and a rock of offense" (I Peter 2:8), in our day offending someone has become the ultimate offence, and so, afraid to offend, we mute the message.

The Spirit of God alone removes the offense through the application of the objective truths of the Word of God—but that's the very thing that many post-conservative Christians are watering down in their music. Little wonder Christians look, sound, and act like the world—instead of the reverse.

LOOK AT ME!

Visiting a church one Sunday morning, I led my family cautiously through a minefield of microphone wires and amp chords to our seats—just beneath a suspended speaker the size of a piano. My kids stared wide-eyed at the bongo drums, the Starbucks coffee in nearly every hand, the female worship leaders and androgynous-seeming males on stage in their Hawaiian shirts. One of my young sons leaned over and whispered, "Is this an entertainment show?"

One thing is indisputable: this kind of ethos in Christian worship is modelled after the entertainment industry. Of course, they're using entertainment as a means to an end: evangelism. Most church leaders want to get them in the door by entertaining them with a really good band. But is this compatible with the spirit of celebrity seen throughout the entertainment world?

Michael Bloodgood, heavy-metal bassist and founder of the Christian Music Hall of Fame band, "Bloodgood," thinks it is. "We're like Billy Graham with guitars. Rock and roll is neutral. It depends on the spirit."

Check out the album covers of the latest Christian bands if you want to discern the spirit. You'll discover shameless aping of secular musicians: provocative females, metro males, and armed-crossing hauteur. Click on the play button and you will hear desperate mainstream-wannabes posturing to be noticed by secular record labels.

Vanguard of contemporary Christian music, Keith Green, was troubled by the prevailing spirit decades ago, "the 'look at me!' attitude... the 'Can't you see we are as good as the world!' syndrome." I suspect Green would be far more distressed at the spirit he would see if he were alive today.

What British journalist and historian Paul Johnson observed about culture in general, many Christians seem desperate to imitate. "Entertainment [has] displaced traditional culture as the focus of attention, and celebrity has ejected quality as the measure of value."

I DON'T LISTEN TO THE WORDS

Getting the musical cart before the objective-content horse is not simply a contemporary issue. Regardless of musical style, Christians throughout two millennia have known that music was not neutral and that it is a perennial problem of allowing the music to take over, to wag the dog. St. Augustine bemoaned his own tendency to be "more moved by the song than the thing which is sung," and considered reversing the priority a serious sin.

Fast forward a thousand years. Calvin knew that music was not neutral; some songs were "composed merely to tickle and delight the ear." These songs he believed were "unbecoming to the majesty of the Church and cannot but be most displeasing to God." Calvin added strong caution about allowing the ear to guide the mind, a warning we must hear again. "We must beware lest our ears be more intent on the music than our minds on the spiritual meaning of the words."

What would these saints, and a host like them, say about Christian worship today? Their concerns predated the development of instruments and amplification technology designed to create psychological euphoria with loud, penetrating musical noise. Thoughtful Christians, ones who know the danger of imitating the world's priorities, will pose hard questions to themselves. "Does entertainment music draw more attention to itself and to the performers? Is it designed to help me reflect deeply on the objective meaning of the words being sung? Does it awaken discernment or does it distract?" I think the jury is long in. Yet, most Christians refuse to accept the verdict.

What is the universal response when parents ask kids why they listen to secular music with trashy lyrics? "I don't listen to the words." This is partially true, and wholly by design. Amusement music is produced to affect an emotional response from the music itself rather than an intellectual response to the meaning of the words. Which compels the conclusion that entertainment music is probably a poor choice to "renew the minds" of unbelievers.

Odd, isn't it, that the contemporary church would rationalize using pop entertainment music to be a carrier for evangelism, when the very genre itself admittedly distracts us away from listening to the lyrics. One wonders how many entertainment-music-loving church goers also "don't listen to the words"?

WHOSE EVANGELISM

If the modern-day church wants to take seriously the Great Commission and draw people, like Augustine was drawn in, by our worship, specifically singing in worship, then we must pause and listen to wiser counsel than the latest converted bassist.

The venerable J. I. Packer, during whose lifetime all these changes occurred, wrote that "When evangelism is not fed, fertilized and controlled by theology it becomes a stylized performance seeking its effect through manipulative skills rather than the power of vision and the force of truth." More and more of the churches I visit have allowed "a stylized performance" to supplant the ordinary means of grace in their worship—and in their evangelism.

Whatever the mission statement of the church declares, the entertainment ethos sets up an inviable venue that depends more heavily on music to do what only the Spirit and Word of God can do. UK pastor, John Blanchard, exposes the problem of manipulating with music: "Musical conditioning is not the same as the Holy Spirit challenging the mind to think, the spirit to be still, and the heart to be humbled in the presence of God." The best theologians and pastors have understood these dangers for centuries—until now.

Not only a theologian and preacher, Luther, as a musician and poet, knew that music was not neutral; he made a clear distinction between worthy and unworthy music. "We know that the Devil's music is distasteful and insufferable." But many Christians roll their eyes when someone says such an out-of-touch thing like "Rock has always been the Devil's music."

But it was musical innovator, the late David Bowie, who said, "Rock has always been the Devil's music." There's no indicator that this bothered Bowie, who was insistent: "You can't convince me that it isn't. I believe that rock and roll is dangerous." Meanwhile, many Christians keep repeating the mantra, music is neutral; music is neutral. Churches persist in imagining that by using music styles conceived in the various reiterations of the sexual revolution they are merely plundering the Egyptians. It may prove the reverse.

Pastor of Saint Andrew's Chapel and editor of *Table Talk*, Burk Parsons was a founding member of the boy band, Backstreet Boys. He explains why he eventually quit rock and roll. "The world of show business is the world of man-centered entertainment. The foundational philosophy of man-centered entertainment is to do whatever it takes in order to attract millions of fans and to make millions of dollars."

This requires the "entertainment gurus" to track all the latest cultural fads and follow the "whims and fancies" of the music-listening public, like many candidly admit doing. Parsons continues, "This has become the philosophy of many evangelicals [who] have exchanged God-centered worship for man-centered entertainment that is founded upon the ever-changing principles of the culture rather than upon the unchanging principles of the Word of God." He calls us to worship according to the Word of God, "which transcends the current trends of modern culture."

Pounding the same well-intentioned drum, practitioners of entertainment worship persist in telling the rest of us that to be relevant and reach the culture for Christ we need to get with it and change over to entertainment music. One does wonder how Spurgeon, Calvin, Edwards, or Luther did it before electric guitars.

Zealous church planters are correct about the power of loud entertainment music to change people. Decades ago, rocker Jimi Hendrix understood this. "Music is a spiritual thing of its own. You can hypnotize people with the music and when you get them at their weakest point you can preach into the subconscious what you want to say."

London preacher Martyn Lloyd-Jones, who witnessed the leading decades of these changes, wrote concerning music's power, "We can become drunk on music. Music can have the effect of creating an emotional state in which the mind is no longer functioning as it should be, and no longer discriminating."

The Apostle Paul knew that sinners needed renewed minds to repent and believe the gospel, and they needed renewed minds in order to worship in spirit and in truth, with awe and with reverence. I wonder if some churches now lean on music to do what only the Holy Spirit can do: woo sinners by changing their mind and will, not by first altering their emotions, but by drawing them by the power of the Word to repentance and faith in Christ.

CULTURE WAR

When we pause and take a closer look at worship music informed by the entertainment model, a number of concerning features emerge: There's an over-familiarity and sentimentalism; there's the tendency to bring God down to man's level; there's the fact that the lyrics are written by young people who are musicians first, rather than poetry written by experienced, gifted Christians with theological and literary training; there's the tendency to sing about what we're singing about; there's the simplistic repetitiveness; there's lack of biblical progression of thought; and there's the dumbing-down of the message in order to fit it into the entertainment ethos.

All of these can tend to have a particularly negative effect on at least one demographic of today's church. There may be a connection with churches having fewer men in attendance, as many studies have shown for several decades. Unpopular as it is to point out—even felonious—in these decades there has been what some have called a feminization of Christian worship. Evidence of this is seen in many pernicious ways but perhaps nowhere more uncomfortably for Christian young men than in singing.

In the ethos of entertainment worship, the girls stand caressing the air with their hands, then opening and clenching their hands with the beat, swaying with the pounding rhythm of the music, their voices hushed and breathy, eyes pinched closed, emoting along with the worship leaders. At the risk of over generalizing, this kind of participation seems to come much more easily to women than to men.

What are most men doing? Cleaning their fingernails. Shuffling their feet uncomfortably. Looking for the exit signs. Many men are embarrassed by the public display of emotions, and embarrassed—or allured—by the provocative outfits and yearning posture of some of the female vocalists.

Christine Rosen in the *Wall Street Journal* committed the unpardonable journalistic sin of connecting plummeting male church attendance with the growing number of women taking leadership roles in church. Author Steve Farrar decried the "feminization of our boys" in entertainment worship. "Am I in a church or a spa?" he asked. "At a deal like that, you don't bring your Bible, you bring your moisturizer."

Female journalist for *GQ* magazine embedded in a NYC mega-church reported that the songs had "melodies that all resemble one another… like spa music."

In his book *Why Men Hate Going to Church*, David Murrow argues that because contemporary worship is "tilted toward the feminine heart, created for sensitive women and soft-hearted men to meet Jesus," a masculine man feels emasculated, "like he has to check his testosterone at the sanctuary door."

In the canon of classic hymns, however, men for centuries have sung of battles and fighting, of conquest and triumph, in short, of the manly Christian themes found in the Psalms and the Prophets in Holy Scripture.

"But today's praise songs are mainly love songs to Jesus," wrote Murrow, offering the example, "Hold me close, let your love surround me… I'm desperate without you… Jesus, I'm so in love with you." Another song one of my writing students gave me begins, "Your love is extravagant; your friendship—mmmm—intimate." These "Jesus-is-my-girlfriend" songs, as one author dubbed them, represent a genre that usually says very little about the atoning work of Christ, and reduces him with language more in keeping with an on-line crush.

A recent study on the Contemporary Christian Music industry found that the single greatest demographic of consumers of the two billion albums, singles, music videos, and digital tracks sold were twenty-five to forty-four-year-old women. It's little wonder that an industry producing a product far more appealing to women than to men would have the unintended result of alienating many Christian men.

It is difficult for real Christian men to join in with gusto on lyrics shaped by glam rock and bubblegum pop, and the other vicissitudes of popular music genre churches try on and off with the ever-changing musical trends.

A serious Christian man is bewildered. At an East Coast city church, I sat in the front row during the musical performance, awaiting my turn on the stage to exhort from God's Word. The hip music leader, in skinny jeans and a man bun, was smack-dab in front of me, urging me to participate in ways that made me feel uncomfortable. What I had prepared to preach seemed so out of place in such a setting.

Effeminate men and female worship leaders can make the rest of us feel unspiritual if we don't sing and behave like they do on the stage. And what about Christian young men viewing all this? One frustrated pastor bluntly told the teen males in his church, "you don't have to be a girlie man to be a godly man."

Christians have always been called to be countercultural. We are engaged in every generation of the Church in a war—a culture war. The solution for

Christians in every generation and every formulation of the cultural revolt against God's will and way, is to thoroughly saturate ourselves and our children, our young men and women, in the Word of God and all that it says about being a man and a woman, and all that it declares to us about how we are to worship God in the splendor of his holiness.

To do so, will require us to break ranks with the priorities of our entertainment-driven culture, and it will come at a price. But we will find with Samuel Rutherford and hymn writer Anne Cousin when we arrive at Emmanuel's land that it will have been "a well-spent journey, though seven deaths lay between."

9

LITURGICAL FIDGET

One of my former students, now a married adult and mother, was recently diagnosed with ADHD. She was telling my wife about it and said, "If I've got it, Mr. Bond's got it bad." When I told my mother, she chuckled. "We knew you had something. We just didn't call it that, back then."

My wife calls my latest writing projects or improvements on the farm, "Daddy's manias." So, maybe there's something to it. Though it's likely bothered others more than I've realized (ask my wife), I prefer thinking that it provides the drive that helps me get some things accomplished.

But as I've gotten older my tendencies to be easily distracted have increased. For example, when I'm in a church service where there's a band and instruments stretching across the stage (the capitulation to the entertainment ethos means many churches unblushingly call it the stage), as I attempt to sing, I find my mind darting from the lights to the mounds of cords, then to the shimmering instruments, and then to the performers singing, swaying, crooning, strumming, and drumming on the stage.

Meanwhile, the words on the screens (screens are not good for people with ADHD) seem to me to be far from the most important part of what we're supposed to be doing. It may be the sense that something is out of proportion that makes performers keep repeating the words over and over again. Maybe they think that vain repetition will help us cut through all the distractions and get at the meaning of the words. It's not working for me.

EMPTY PHRASES

How vastly different vain repetition, or the heaping up of empty phrases (Matthew 6:7) is from biblical repetition. Some hasten to object, "Wait, what about repetition in the Psalms?" There is repetition of phrases in some psalms, for example, Psalm 136 begins, "Give thanks to the Lord, for he is good, for his steadfast love endures forever." Twenty-six times the psalmist reminds us that "his steadfast love endures forever."

So, what's wrong with repetition? We repeat to remember, don't we? And here it is, right there on the pages of God's Word, repetition. What's more, you have the same refrain five time over in Psalm 118. So, why are some critics so concerned about the repetitiveness of contemporary worship lyrics?

Because there is a vast difference between how the inspired psalmists use repetition and how the uninspired contemporary musician uses it.

The foundations of Anglo-Saxon aesthetic are unity and progression. Whatever the artistic genre, you need both unity and progression for things to work. Poets and composers have understood this for centuries—until the last generation or so. The psalmists employ both unity and progression. Most contemporary lyricists do not.

Notice the unity and progression of Psalm 136:4, "to him who alone does great wonders, for his steadfast love endures forever." What follows for the next twenty-two verses are specific details about the great wonders God has done. Beginning with God creating the heavens, the earth, the water, the great lights, the sun, the moon, and so forth, the psalmist skillfully punctuates his developed progression of details about those wonders with the unity of refrain: "his steadfast love endures forever." The progression intensifies as the psalmist shifts to rehearsing the history of redemption of God's children, with specific details of that history, right down to God striking down "Og, king of Bashan" (20). Here, the refrain serves to punctuate the richly developed progression of the Psalm.

Moreover, it is important to observe, for all who want to be biblical, that Psalm 136 and Psalm 118 are all there is; few if any other psalms use what could be called a repetitive refrain. Two out of 150 psalms. In the divinely inspired hymnal of the old covenant there are only 1.33% of psalms that employ a refrain. We should be cautious about heaping up phrases, using repetition in our praying or in our singing, and, it would be safe to conclude that the Bible is demonstrating that repetition ought never to be of the vain and empty sort (Matthew 6:7).

VAIN REPETITION

How unlike the vacuous repetition of much that passes for music in worship in the majority of Christian churches today. Contrast the inspired unity and progression of Psalm 136 with Jesus Culture's lyric "Set Fire."

> Set a fire down in my soul
> That I can't contain and I can't control,
> 'Cause I want more of you, God,
> I want more of you, God

As near as I could count, with nothing that resembles progression of thought, these empty lines are repeated eighteen times; that's assuming the music leader doesn't feel moved to want you to want to sing more of them. Not only a trend-setting example of vapid repetition, "Set Fire" illustrates the narcissism, the horizontal posture of much of this material. In this case, the lyric is all about what I want. God is merely an object to satisfy my desires. The focus on my experience, my wants, so frequently featured throughout the genre, stands in sharp contrast with the biblical ethos of worship which is always about what God wants from us, rendered with reverence and awe.

Furthermore, there's a reason why contemporary Christian musicians resort to repetition. It's a simple one, tried and tested. Repetition will help get your song on the charts. After an extensive study of thousands of pop songs from the last fifty years, USC professor Joseph Nunez concluded, "the more you repeated the chorus, the more word repetition, the less complex the song, the better it did."

Finger firmly on the pulse of the secular pop music industry, the Christian music industry has realized the same thing. "Close your eyes and repeat, repeat, repeat," said Michael John Warren, director of a documentary film on Australian mega-church Hillsong. "They do design it to get you in this zone." Warren concluded, "It's almost like a form of meditation."

To get their congregations in the meditative zone, worship leaders pattern the music component of the service to look like and sound like the commercial CCM industry. It's little wonder there's so much repetition and so little content in what passes for Christian lyrics in many churches. It's what gets your song on the charts. It's what sells. Transplant the entertainment ethos into church worship, and it gets people in the zone, helps them achieve the altered state of consciousness, the spiritual high.

One woman in her thirties whose entire Christian experience was of the contemporary worship variety, looking back, wrote, "I realized that the spiritual highs I reached in communal worship were emotionally manufactured through repetitive, vapid, theologically empty music." Like her, there is now an entire generation of Christians who have no other experience; they only know the ethos of entertainment which has supplanted biblical worship throughout their lifetimes. She concluded, "We need music that doesn't simply invoke an orgiastic ecstasy with God. We need music that challenges and takes the theology we sing of seriously."

LET'S MAKE HYMNS COOL

We should applaud the genuine efforts made to return to more substantive content in sung worship. For example, there's a trend among what has been called the Young, Restless, and Reformed movement to recover hymn singing, of a sort. But I've discovered in my own observations that most YRR hipster churches have a rather narrow repertoire of hymns.

Traditional hymn melodies stretch the ability of many contemporary musicians and require many hours of rehearsal, which insures the repertoire will be vastly smaller than the expansive body of hymns on many biblical themes, written over many centuries, that used to be contained in a book called a hymnal, ready to hand in front of every worshiper.

Unlike the ordinary means of grace that informed the liturgy used throughout the centuries, in contemporary worship there is usually little or no connection linking the themes of the hymns with the other components of Christian worship, including even the sermon topic. Churches that do this may find themselves singing a narrow cycle of songs over and over, usually with little or no thematic connection to the rest of the worship.

The handful of classic hymns from the Reformation and the Great Awakening in the repertoire are heavily edited, with ample refrains and repetition of lines, and are usually set to new, breathy, emotive tunes. In other words, the lead musician is desperately trying to configure the hymn to sound and feel more like the contemporary-worship-song genre, and less like psalms and hymns and how congregations of God's people have been singing them for two millennia.

Moreover, music leaders require us to stop singing and listen to frequent instrumental bridges between lines, presumably for emotional effect. However clever and musically cool these bridges are, the start-and-stop rhythm they create are like a runner in a race, just when getting his stride, momentum moving forward, suddenly a dog bolts across the track, breaking the runner's stride, forcing him to stop and start up again. But just for a minute. Check out this cool riff. This singing-stopping pattern retards congregational participation because it confuses and deflates those of us trying to sing.

Try singing Luther's "A Mighty Fortress," but with awkward, emotive pauses between lines that are intended, I am sure, to lead me to contemplation. Just as we had a full lung of oxygen, eager to launch forward, "Let goods and kindred go—" the leader veers off and strums an instrumental bridge. I've caught myself continuing, "This mortal life also,/The body they may kill…"

Silly me. What am I trying to do? Take over the singing? Embarrassed, I proceed with a great deal more caution in my voice. Soon enough, I settle in to a hesitant, tuneless murmuring, like most everyone else around me, that is, those who are actually singing. It's safer that way. Who knows what innovation lurks around the next corner?

Yet more disturbing are the emotive ejaculations from the singers during those frequent bridges. Eyes pinched shut, faces contorted with feeling. One secular journalist looking on concluded that "contemporary worship services, with their hands in the air, gyrating bodies, and closed eyes, resembled orgasm." But these are the music leaders, demonstrating for us how we ought to do it, presumably how they think God ought to do it. I glance around the room. This is difficult to do for most of us. So, we let them do it for us.

This kind of performance-based leading stifles participation and disunifies the Church. Certainly, recover singing the great hymns. But it would be better if they didn't tamper with them. They're great for a reason, and new lines, refrains, bridges, stanzas added by a young, zealous music leader will far more likely cheapen what has already demonstrated through the centuries its great worth to the people of God.

Instead of taking advantage of the opportunity to lift the congregation out of our contemporary, narcissistic moment and unite our hearts and voices with what the saints have been singing for centuries, we intrude, we presume to improve, we assert ourselves to fix the deficiencies of the grand lyrics that have united the people of God in worship for ages.

LITURGICAL FIDGIT

"If it works, don't fix it." Tampering with what already works is a staple of the contemporary church. Some changes are made specifically to accommodate cultural changes, to make the contemporary church and her worship seem more relevant. But some changes are made simply to stop doing it the way Christians have been doing it, to distance today's churches from the fuddy-duddy churches of the past. Churches, dissatisfied with the ordinary means of grace, cast about for something new and exciting to show the world that modern Christians can be with it, up-to-date, cool, and hip.

What goes around comes around, and attempting to update the Church and her worship had come around in C. S. Lewis's day. Eager revisionists were once again sharpening their knives to update the Anglican confessional and liturgical standards.

Frustrated by this, Lewis wrote in his book *Letters to Malcom, Chiefly on Prayer*, "It looks as if they believed people can be lured to go to church by incessant abridgments [and] simplifications of the service." Lewis was pretty convinced revision always degraded worship, especially if it was change for its own sake. "Novelty, simply as such, can have only an entertainment value."

Lewis knew what the contemporary church seems to have entirely forgotten: mature and thoughtful Christians don't go to church to be entertained. Worship ought so to direct our minds to God that the minister, the building, the stain glass, the bright lights, the fog machine, the other worshipers, the liturgy itself disappear and only God remains.

"Every novelty prevents this," Lewis argues. "It fixes our attention on the service itself, and thinking about worship is a different thing from worshiping." He urged caution on making changes and revising the liturgy because "It is easy to break eggs without making omelets. The good to be done by revision needs to be very great and very certain before we throw that away." All the uncertainty and newness of the changes, he concluded, "lays one's devotion waste."

So often changes are made by pastors and musicians who are not lacking in zeal, or desire to reach the lost, but they are lacking in the wisdom that comes from experience; many of the champions of change are lacking in theological training, in extensive reading in Church history, in what the wisest theologians of the past have taught about worship and about singing in worship, and almost all of these change agents are lacking in literary training and skill, and a number of music leaders are lacking in formal musical training, especially music education thoroughly informed by sound theology.

Lewis wished these revision-minded church leaders in his own day remembered that the Lord charged Peter to "Feed my sheep," not "Try experiments on my rats, or even, teach my performing dogs new tricks." He concludes with a call for "permanence and uniformity" in the worship service. He calls the love of novelty and revision the "Liturgical fidget" of the Church. Finally, if revision is needed, he believed it should be "here a little and there a little; one obsolete word replaced in a century."

Imagine what Lewis would say about the devolution of the "Liturgical fidget" as seen in contemporary worship today. We've managed to make massive changes, to overhaul sung worship by the truckload, and all in half a century.

IT'S ALL ABOUT THE MUSIC

Worship is now synonymous with music. When someone says "The worship was, like, so awesome this morning," what they mean is the band was playing right on. The music made them feel good. And by music, they primarily mean the coordination of instruments and the solo voice of the music leader and other vocalists. It was an awesome performance. What they likely are not considering is the united voice of the congregation, "teaching and admonishing one another," as they lift their full voice in sung praises to God.

They may not even be thinking very much about the sermon, the Word preached in Christ's pulpit. I overheard a telling exchange after a service I attended at a hipster church.

"Do you make recordings?" a woman asked the sound technicians.

"Of the band? No, we don't." He sounded really bummed about it.

The woman tried again. "Uh, I meant of the sermon?"

It took the sound tech a minute to process her request. "Oh, that."

The priority of music over message, instruments over lyrical and theological content, electronic sound over the voice of the congregation, has an accumulative result that erodes and contradicts biblical worship, the best of intentions, notwithstanding.

"Too much of our Sunday morning worship," observed Jared C. Wilson, "sets the cart of affections before the horse of belief." When we do this, we are asking our affections to do what they are not capable of doing. The emotive is not capable of lifting us to the contemplative, because our feelings very often overwhelm contemplation. It's what unregulated feelings do.

Music-driven worship presumes to begin with appealing to our emotions to elevate us to deeper thinking. But it never works that way. We must first have light, doctrinal truth, before we can experience true doxological heat. Begin with emotionally concocted heat, we will never get to light. Only the renewed mind can produce the inflamed heart, a heart inflamed by Christ himself and not by cheap-trick, musical manipulation of the emotions.

"You are what you sing," wrote Daniel Block. "Shallow theology will produce shallow music, and shallow music will produce shallow theology." There is a connection; the medium truly is the message, or a significant part of it.

One of the main reasons for a less-complex message in the lyrics sung in churches today is that the monotone of the pop entertainment ethos requires a lesser message. Even if the lyrical content is there, it is subsumed by the dominant medium; the pop musical sound simply cannot bear the weight of the words.

Compared with the nuanced range of historic melodies the Church has sung, popular music structures simply do not have the breadth and range to carry the depth of biblical content that used to be on our lips as we sang in worship. The ubiquitous evidence is the banality of the amusement culture itself. There's a fairly narrow range of human emotions capable of being aroused by popular music. Rock and roll and its derivations are good at invoking recklessness but fall short of deeper reckoning; they are good at trivializing the stupendous while making the trivial seem astounding; it is music that more easily vulgarizes than ennobles, enervates than instills courage. But it's washing down *beouf bourguignon* with Kool-Aid to wed the deep truths of redemption with music designed to amuse and entertain.

The performance ethos itself bars us from contemplation of the deeper mysteries so comprehensively explored in the psalms and best hymns of the centuries. Appropriately, that lyrical richness was carried and undergirded with melodies and instrumental arrangements appropriate to the spiritual and theological depth of the words that Christians have been taking on their lips in song for two millennia—until now.

10

FILET MIGNON AND CHERRY COKE

Beautiful music," said Luther, "is one of the most magnificent and delightful presents God has given us." Polarized as we are over what music qualifies as beautiful, I do wonder what Luther would have to say after he had a good listen to some of our sung worship today.

In the last fifty years church music has undergone a radical metamorphosis. While most Christians applaud these unprecedented changes, I sometimes feel like many efforts to blend the timeless truths of the gospel of Jesus Christ with pop music modeled after the entertainment industry work about as well as pairing *filet mignon* with Cherry Coke.

Not surprisingly, in response to the tendency of worship leaders to prefer music composed in the last fifty years, there are those who want to recover the beauty of what is often termed classical music.

I have the highest regard for composers of great music like Bach and Beethoven, Mendelssohn and Mahler (and Luther); my music collection and listening preferences are heavily weighted toward musical luminaries like these.

I can listen to the cello suites of J. S. Bach incessantly. It sounds to my ear, in so many of his works, like Bach has managed to strike the chord of eternity. I've stood in his home in Eisenach, Germany listening to his *St. Matthew's Passion*, and felt that Bach, the unapologetic Christian, may have more perfectly lived out his theology in his music than any other artist. "I play the notes as they are written," wrote Bach, "but it is God who makes the music." Placing the initials SDG, *soli Deo Gloria* at the end of all his compositions, "secular or sacred," was not perfunctory for Bach. He truly did believe it was "God who makes the music."

Others have expressed their appreciation far better. Pablo Casals, Catalan cellist, composer, and conductor, regarded by many as the greatest cellist of all time, put it this way, "To make divine things human, and human things divine; such is J. S. Bach, the greatest and purest moment in music of all time." A man of prodigious musical acclaim in his own right, Casals could not help speaking in religious terms about the music of Bach.

Perhaps there's no better reason for this than Bach's own intentionality as a Christian who acknowledged that his gift of music was a gift of God to be offered back in the service and honor of God. As Aleksandr Solzhenitsyn put it, "It is the artist who realizes that there is a supreme force above him and works gladly away as a small apprentice under God's heaven."

Wouldn't it be wonderful if more artists, poets, and musicians thought this way about their gifts? How I would love to see another generation of God's people develop a renewed appreciation of the splendor and beauty of music that strikes the chord of eternity in worship. But I wonder if our zeal to bring this about at times consumes our wisdom.

GAZING ON THE MUSIC

In my church experiences over the years, I have found myself jolted out of meditation on the living God in worship by a liturgy feature that worries me. While I attempt to take the words of the silent prayer to heart—"Turn my heart to you, O Lord."—I am deftly steered clear of that by a prominent text identifying the music being played, "Prelude in B-flat major, Felix Mendelssohn Bartholdy (1809-1847)." To be blunt, it strikes me as intrusively academic and, dare I say it, elitist, to be confronted with this information so prominently in the liturgical guide to worship. While attempting to quiet my heart before the Lord in preparation for worship, I am diverted by details straight from the syllabus of a music appreciation course.

Furthermore, I wonder how it strikes an unbelieving visitor. There's already plenty of high register elements surrounding an unbeliever in Christian worship, and then we club him with this wholly unnecessary one. Whereas the music itself might have helped lift him above the ordinary and commonplace, the labeling in the bulletin creates a Berlin Wall, one that in all likelihood will appear to be a snub. "We are a sophisticated church of elite music snobs," the labeling appears to be saying. "You're welcome here if you become one too."

HIGH-BROW MEDITATIONS

For believer or unbeliever, the placarding of the music and composer has shifted us from high thoughts of God to high-brow thoughts of Western art music. The prominent music labeling in the bulletin reminds me of the derailing distraction that happens in a liturgy where worshipers are pointed to a sculpture or painting of Jesus instead of to Jesus himself. Calvin was right we he observed that "...every one of us is, even from his mother's womb, a master craftsman of idols."

The prominence of the music and the composer is made still more preeminent by what is sometimes left out. Oddly, in some bulletins we do not identify the author of the poetry in the hymns—Newton or Cowper, Watts or Wesley—yet we contort ourselves placarding the music and composer. Oddly, as I prepare to sing, "Take my life and let it be / Consecrated Lord to thee," I am confronted with the important fact that Franz Liszt who was born in 1811 and who died in 1886 wrote the music *Consolation* being now played by the musician, while the poet who penned the words we're singing, Frances Havergal, is never mentioned.

WORDS COME FIRST

But what's so wrong with drawing attention to the music and the composer? After all, in the opening

154

pages of Genesis (4:21) it says that "Jubal was the father of all who play the lyre and pipe." And we learn about the Sons of Korah and their important role as musicians and composers of music for worship. And don't some psalms lead off telling us the actual name of the tune, for example, "Doe of the Dawn" (22)? What's the problem? It's all right there in the Bible?

The problem is precisely because it isn't all right there in the Bible, not in the way it is in some of our printed worship guides. In the Bible the music is only rarely identified in the inspired liturgy of the psalms. While the vast majority of the psalms identify the poet who, under divine inspiration, wrote the poetry of the psalm, very few of the 150 psalms identify the name of the tune, and fewer still identify the musical composer. What's more, the smartest Old Testament scholar on the planet does not have a clue what "Doe of the Dawn" sounded like; as much as me may wish they had, not a riff from an original psalm tune has survived—but every jot and tittle of the *words* of 150 psalms has.

Why are the psalms so frequently attributed to the poets but so seldom to the musicians? Likely it is because Christianity is all about the Word of God, revealed to us in a book filled with words, including the most glorious poetry ever penned. While "...music is one of the most magnificent and delightful presents God has given us," and ought to have a central place in Christian worship, the Bible and Christian worship is first and last all about the words.

The way some of our worship guides identify music and text, however, one would think it were the reverse. Music comes first, the words come after. Whatever we claim our priorities are in worship, looking at the order of service in some bulletins on a Sunday morning and it feels like this: "Turn my heart to the *Sonata quasi una Fantasia* Op 27. No. 2, O Lord, and turn me to Ludwig van Beethoven, and to his birth year in 1770 and to the year of his death in 1827, O Lord." When we do this, our zeal to recover classical music has become the Cherry Coke of the metaphor.

THE SOLUTION

In the interest of doing everything we do in word and deed as we sing psalms, hymns, and spiritual songs in the name of Jesus (Colossians 3:16-17), a Christ-centered liturgy would do well to include neither the composer's name nor the poet's name in the progression through the printed guide to worship.

Let's stop thinking of our printed liturgy as a polemic on our theology of worship in which we showcase our sophisticated classical music taste. If we do choose to identify artists, we would do well to be psalm-like in our priority, never subordinating poetry and poet to musical composition and composer. The simplest solution? Identify hymn writers and composers in footnotes at the end of the bulletin—back page, small print, after the announcements and notifications.

It seems to me that would be more in keeping with how J. S. Bach concluded his compositions: *soli Deo Gloria.*

POP MUSICIAN FIRST

It's so much more fun to point out the fallacies of the other guys, but how do those committed to an entertainment-modeled worship placard their priorities? Google search almost any hymn, and you will see the name of a contemporary musician as the "songwriter" attached to the lyric of a long-dead hymn writer. Some may still know that Isaac Watts wrote the hymn, or Robert Robinson, or the ancient Irish poet who wrote "Be Thou My Vision" (or the scholar/translator Mary E. Bryne, or poet Eleanor H. Hull who gave us the English poetry). But it is the height of arrogance, not to mention brazen plagiarism, to credit a modern musician who worked out the guitar chords (all three of them) and did a YouTube video of himself singing the magisterial lyric of any hymn writer, alive or dead.

Why do so many contemporary musicians so shamelessly do this? Firstly, because the poetry now lies in the public domain, so they feel like it's up for grabs. The poet who wrote it is dead. Besides, they added a repeat of the final line (which may be repeated eleven times—or more, if the Spirit moves). And in many cases, they have helped the dead poet by replacing his inferior lines with their more up-to-date ones, and added their own refrain, not to mention those frequent instrumental bridges that the congregation is supposed to stop singing and listen to. After all that, the original poetry was merely raw material, and so, they now place their name, even their copyright, on the hymn.

Secondly, I think the reason contemporary musicians and worship leaders feel so free to place their name as the songwriter, usually not even mentioning the original

157

poet, is because they are musicians. They're not poets, not by any credible definition that has stood the test of more than a nanosecond in the literary timeline. They are, first and last, musicians, performers, and, to their credit, they did the performance.

Whatever the rationale, the poetry is subordinate to the music. The contemporary musician feels that the lyrics are malleable, there to be shaped to what fits the music best, in their judgment, according to their tastes. This has sometimes led to, after a zealous musician gets his hands on it, nothing short of the abject slaughter of some of the finest poetry penned.

TUNEFUL FOOLS

I find myself in many different churches, some of them arranged with musicians, instruments front and center, the main room lights dimmed, with colored flood lighting behind and sometimes on the musicians—arranged for entertainment, like the stage at a pop music concert.

In the entertainment arrangement, worship is the music, not the content of the lyrics being sung, but the music. When we hear, "The worship was so, like, awesome this afternoon," this is code for: the band was really hitting their stride today. The music was awesome.

What is going on, here? Long before our current "liturgical fidget," Neoclassical poet Alexander Pope observed those who preferred music over doctrinal and lyrical content. He called them "tuneful fools" who only admired the music, who cared only "to please the ear,

> Not mend their minds; as some to church repair,
> Not for the doctrine, but the music there."

Pope is using satire to highlight the objective content priority; if our praise is genuine, acceptable to God, we will be moved to that praise more from the objective truths in the poetry than from the emotion generated by the music itself. This ought to make sense to both factions, those who want classical music and those who insist on pop entertainment music.

If 300 years ago there was the danger of some people going to church for the music and not for the words being sung, how much more so in a technologically advanced day when the decibels are hundreds of times the volume achieved by acoustical instruments in any other historical moment since creation.

THE SAME SOLUTION

The solution, as always, is to return to the Bible. Specifically, to the psalms, which were clearly intended for singing. Though David was a poet and a musician who played the harp, it is significant, however, that only the lyric of the psalms survives in the canon of Scripture.

There are indicators in a few psalms that may refer to specific musical settings for the texts. Part of the inspired text of Psalm 89, for example, is a superscription that reads "A Maskil of Ethan the Ezrahite." Hebrew scholars don't seem to know exactly what a Maskil was. Is it referring to a type of musical setting or to a more contemplative prayer? Other psalms indicate the words were to be sung to "Lilies" or "Lilies of the Covenant," but nobody knows what the ancient tune "Lilies" sounded like. There's no indication whatsoever about the musical sound. Several psalms have instruction in the superscription about "The Gittith." What is a Gittith? Once again, scholars do not seem to know for sure. It may be a musical term or may even refer to a musical instrument. Though it is there in the superscription of the psalm, we do not know what it means for sure, or what it sounded like.

There are several important implications from these facts. The most obvious and important being that lyric takes precedent over music. I do not doubt that ancient Hebrew music was beautiful and appropriate to the lyric. But, clearly, the Holy Spirit did not believe that those ancient melodies were essential to the use of the psalms. What was of paramount importance was the words. The inspired, God-breathed words.

Our culture of music entertainment has this entirely reversed. Whereas, most of the psalms indicate who wrote the words of the specific psalm, only a few of them are credited to the Sons of Korah, a few tell us who did the music; none tell us who was singing or who was playing the harp.

Search YouTube for "Amazing Grace" and you will think that it must have been written by Alan Jackson or Gary Downey—or any number of other performers of John Newton's well-loved hymn.

I experienced this when my Rise & Worship album was released in 2017. The YouTube versions of each of my hymns appeared with the name of the composer of the tunes and the lead performer singing on the cd, but none of those videos mentioned who actually wrote the lyric, the poetry. That may simply sound like sour grapes, like I want the glory and the musicians stole it from me. I sincerely hope that is not the case. I want to be more like J. S. Bach and give all the glory to God for anything I write. When it's all said and done, I want to work "gladly away as a small apprentice under God's heaven."

At best, Christians should want to credit what we produce today the way the psalms do, with priority on the words. The most biblical, word-centered way of crediting would be in the order of creation: lyric, melody, then who sings it.

Google "Come Thou Fount" and you will immediately read that Chris-somebody is the songwriter, not Robert Robinson. The musician Chris-somebody has absconded with Robinson's original hymn lyric.

Come thou Fount of every blessing
Tune my heart to sing thy grace;
Streams of mercy, never ceasing,
Call for songs of loudest praise.
Teach me some melodious sonnet,
Sung by flaming tongues above.
Praise the mount! I'm fixed upon it,
Mount of God's unchanging love.

Rich with biblical allusions, it is a masterful work of sacred poetry, yet I am certain that Robert Robinson, if he somehow knows about the blatant plagiarism, is not troubled in the least. But we ought to be, if for no other reason, than for the sake of accurately connecting this generation of Christians with their true family the Church throughout the ages.

Robinson believed that such never-ceasing streams of mercy "Call[ed] for songs of loudest praise." Songs— loud songs—sung by the full voice of the people of God, joining their voices with the "flaming tongues above."

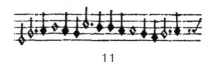

11

DOXOLOGY FOR ALL TIME

It was an autumn Sunday evening in 1976 when, as a seventeen-year-old, the gospel of grace alone through faith alone in Christ alone became irrevocably real to my soul. I remember it vividly: the awakened hearing of truths I had been tenderly taught since my earliest recollections, the sense of wonder at divine grace, and the experiential thrill of the reality of the cross and of Christ my Savior shedding his blood, suffering and dying in my place, for my sin and my guilt. I remember hot tears stinging my cheeks as the genuineness of grace and the gospel washed over me that evening.

With a trembling hand and a heart nearly bursting with love and gratitude for the free grace of God, I reached for the elements of bread and wine, Christ therein pictured, symbolized, and made spiritually real before me.

What was the means that awakened a young man that glorious evening? Was it an entertaining sermon delivered by a celebrity preacher? Was it the emotional hype concocted by the latest Christian rock band? Was it high church ceremony attempting to fabricate the transcendent? No, it was none of these.

It was Isaac Watts.

I had sung the words of his hymn at Communion every month for eleven years, but that evening, Watts' rich poetry dazzled my imagination and made a deep and lasting impression on my heart. It's not cool at seventeen to weep publicly, but I wept, and while I did, I managed to join Watts in his slack-jawed wonder at the cross.

> When I survey the wondrous cross
> On which the Prince of glory died,
> My richest gain I count but loss,
> And pour contempt on all my pride.

By his incomparable imagination, Watts transported me back to hot, dusty Golgotha, where I heard the thudding of the hammer on the spikes, the taunting and spitting, the moaning and wails of sorrow. With Watts' words, I became the young man surveying that wondrous cross. With eyes of faith, I was the one seeing the Prince of glory forsaken by his Father and dying in anguish. And because I was now seeing it, I was the one resolving to count but loss all my aspirations to riches and greatness. I was, for the first time, pouring contempt on all my delusional pride of body and mind.

> Forbid it, Lord, that I should boast,
> Save in the cross of Christ my God:
> All the vain things that charm me most,
> I sacrifice them to his blood.

Watts, by his sense of wonder at the cross of Christ, and with skillful strokes of his poetic pen, showed me the absurdity of my view of the world. He deftly stirred up in me the ugliness and utter inappropriateness of my pride and boasting, my preoccupation with empty things that so captivated my teen world. By vividly holding before me the cross of Jesus, he demanded that I drop everything and reckon with it. By his words, Watts compelled me to join him, to see with him the One who hung on that cross for me.

> See from his head, his hands, his feet,
> Sorrow and love flow mingled down:
> Did e'er such love and sorrow meet,
> Or thorns compose so rich a crown?

Watts' rhetorical question caused me to see how ridiculous my sense of value had been. I had been scrambling after the world's riches, wisdom, and entertainments. But Watts held before me Christ—his head, his hands, his feet—and the surpassing richness of his thorny crown. It was as if I was there and could see it, hear him groaning, and feel the penetration of each thorn in his brow. I was compelled to respond.

> Were the whole realm of nature mine,
> That were a present far too small;
> Love so amazing, so divine,
> Demands my soul, my life, my all.

Watts assaulted my deeply flawed value system with this closing quatrain. How absurd it was for me to think that I could own every piece of wealth in the entire natural world, and then to imagine that I could offer it as a gift, and it would somehow be proportionate to Jesus himself. With a few strokes of his quill, Watts smashed all that for me. His imaginative comparison of all the temporal riches of nature heaped up as a present on one side, and the atoning sacrifice of Jesus Christ for my sins on the other, shamed me; it made me "hide my blushing face while his dear cross appeared."

In sixteen short lines of poetry, in 128 syllables, Watts demolished my twisted sense of value and drove me to my knees at the foot of that cross. He had peeled back the glitter of the temporal world, had parted the clouds with his pen, and in that parting he had dazzled me with divine love, love so amazing that it demanded my soul, my life, my all—every part of me belonged to Jesus. He purchased my life on that cross, and such amazing love for me graciously drew me, irresistibly compelled me, to want more than anything to forsake all else and follow Jesus.

WHY ISAAC WATTS?

As a consequence of having my spiritual imagination baptized by Watts' imagination, he has long held an important place in my mind and heart. When my devotion is cold and stale in public or in private, I turn to Watts, who "give[s] me the wings of faith" and turns me to Jesus. I'm inclined to think that if Watts, more than two hundred years after his death, can be the means of awakening the soul of a seventeen-year-old young man, there just may be a great deal in his body of work that no generation of Christians can afford to live without.

First, we need Watts' poetry in our lives. Our world clambers after the latest thing, and as we wear ourselves out in the process, great poets such as Watts often get put in a box on the curb for the thrift store pick-up. How could a gawky, male poet, living and writing three hundred years ago, be relevant today? Our postmodern, post-Christian, post-biblical culture has almost totally dismissed what was called poetry in Watts' day. Few deny it: ours is a post-poetry culture.

One tragic result of 19th century Transcendentalism abandoning poetic form and celebrating unbridled individualism is that we have forfeited the ability to measure the quality of poetry. Gaseous exhibitionism proliferates; emotive self-referentialism rules the poetic day. Many well-intentioned worship leaders know nothing else; in the two or three decades of their lives, this is their only experience of poetry. Many who lead music in their church have never heard Watts express his poetic purpose:

> Begin, my tongue, some heav'nly theme,
> And speak some boundless thing.
> The mighty works, or mightier Name
> Of our eternal King.

While Watts had made the name of our eternal King the theme of his poetry, ours is a literary world without a rudder, where poetry has no boundaries, no canvas, no walls, no arches, no vaulted ceilings—and, hence, no enduring grandeur because it has no "boundless thing" for its objective.

Today one can create verse and call it poetry by doing a Google search, then blending the results into lines of absurdity. And, yes, it has a name: flarf. Flarf poetry and its derivatives have redefined what poetry is. Redefining is what postmodernity does best, and the result is that the rich literary legacy of the past is on the verge of being forgotten—and Watts with it.

Were he alive today, I doubt that it would occur to Watts to celebrate cyber randomness with his pen—or to write a hymn in celebration of himself like Romantic poet Walt Whitman did in "Song of Myself," wherein he opined that "Nothing, not God is greater... more wonderful than myself." Watts never wrote anything like that.

JUST THINK ABOUT IT

Watts was an extraordinarily gifted poet, one who virtually thought in rhyme and meter, and who wrote most of his poetry in first draft. With such skills, he could have been a leading man of letters in Neoclassical Britain. Watts' era was termed the Age of Johnson, and Samuel Johnson himself ranked Watts among the great authors and said of him, "His ear was well tuned, and his diction was elegant and copious."

Though the University of Edinburgh and the University of Aberdeen conferred on Watts the honor of doctor of divinity degrees in 1728, many literary critics have considered his poetry to be too explicitly Christian for literary acclaim. This was by design. Brilliant poet that he was, Watts avoided, as he termed it, the "excess baggage of intricate form as well as of poetical adornment." His was a gospel objective first and last. Poetry, for Watts, was a means to a higher end, a requirement of all great poetry.

Hence, he was unapologetically a biblical and theological poet who has given to all Christians a rich legacy of sung worship, full of imagination, skill, deep theological perception, vivid sensory insight, cheerfulness in the midst of suffering and disadvantages, and a contagious sense of wonder at the majesty of God. Ours is a world that desperately needs Watts' poetry.

Second, we need Watts' voice in our worship. Christian worship desperately needs Watts. I have sat in worship services with well-meaning Christians singing, "Yes, Lord, yes, Lord, yes, yes, Lord." In another service, I sat bewildered as all around me folks held their hands aloft, caressing the air, singing, "Just think about it, just think about it, just think about it." Not wanting to stand there being the critic, I attempted to get my mind around just what it was I was supposed to be thinking about. Try as I might, I could find little in the words they were singing that required any degree of thought about anything.

I pity a world without Watts. I pity a church without him. Why would Christians want to cut themselves off from rich theological passion skillfully adorned, as in Watts' finest hymns?

In yet another service, I watched others sing Watts' "When I Survey the Wondrous Cross," but I was little moved by the words. As near as I can tell, the reason Watts did not move me this time was that there were many elements in that worship that distracted me from taking the words on my lips and into my heart as my own. The swaying worship leaders and all the paraphernalia of the indie-rock band filled the stage, and the volume was cranked up so loud that I was eventually forced to take my seven-year-old out of the place, his hands clamped tightly over his ears. I watched rather than sang because in this kind of entertainment venue, it matters little whether the congregation participates in the singing. It's fine if they do, of course, but it makes no difference to what one hears. The emotive vocal inflections and the pinched facial contortions of the well-meaning worship leader are difficult for most of us to emulate, and the occasional unexpected repetition of lines or addition of improvised lyrics leaves one singing something other than what the worship leader is singing. Not to worry, no one will hear you anyway.

I stood next to my eldest son in an urban warehouse church in Seattle, Washington, the walls painted black, various colored lighting flashing around the stage and room, the videographer projecting on the screen behind the band a giant close-up of the lead guitarist's fingers sliding up and down the neck of his instrument. Under the assaulting influence of the new nightclub liturgy, I again wondered whether I was supposed to be singing something. There were 2,000 nineteen to twenty-nine-year-olds in the room, but I could not hear anyone singing except the lead guitarist, and he was groaning in a manner I felt intensely uncomfortable attempting to emulate. I turned to my son, took a deep breath, and yelled, "Are we supposed to be singing?" He turned and hollered back in my ear, "I don't know." No one around us was disturbed in the slightest by our exchange.

Just as the medieval church cut off the congregation from participating in the sung worship of the service, today many well-meaning Christian leaders have reconstructed a sung worship wherein congregational participation does not matter. We sit or stand as our medieval forbears did and watch others sing for us. Worship has become a show, amusement, an entertaining means of connecting to the hip youth culture with, ostensibly, the gospel. Such a venue produces a response in the hearer—one super-charged with raw emotion—but I wonder whether it is an emotional response produced by a mind renewed by deep consideration of the objective truths of the gospel of grace or by the music itself.

INFLAME HEARTS

Watts clearly understood all this. He no doubt learned it from the psalms and perhaps from John Calvin's preface to his commentary on the psalms:

> We know by experience that singing has great force and vigor to move and inflame the hearts of men to invoke and praise God with a more vehement and ardent zeal. Care must always be taken that the song be neither light nor frivolous; but that it have weight and majesty, and also, there is a great difference between music which one makes to entertain men at table and in their houses, and the psalms which are sung in the Church in the presence of God and his angels.

In an age of entertainment-driven worship, a recovered appreciation of Watts as a hymn writer is critical to correcting the "light" and "frivolous" tendencies of the postmodern church, and perhaps the dark and edgy ones, too. Every biblically mature generation in the Church will want to contribute poetry and music to the Church's worship—but, alas, so will every biblically immature one. Watts makes an excellent role model to guide the new generations of poets who presume to write lyrics for the corporate worship of God's people.

Instead of letting his son be guided by the transient poetic and music appetites of the moment, Watts' father taught him who must guide his pen:

In ancient times God's worship did accord,
Not with tradition, but the written word;
Himself has told us how he'll be adored.

Watts got his father's message: what Christians sing in worship must be guided by what God has revealed about how we are to sing to such a God. Watts mastered the poetic gift with which he was entrusted and earned the undisputed title "the Father of English Hymnody." If hymns are poems written in praise and adoration of God, then that makes Watts the father of English-speaking praise of God. Every Christian who cares about living a life of praise will want his sung worship to be guided by Watts' heart, mind, and poetic devotion. Why? Because Watts was consumed with wonder at Jesus Christ, the supreme object of Christian worship.

Third, we need Watts' example as we live in our frailty. Yet another important reason for surveying Watts' life and work is that his life is a model of patience in affliction for all Christians who suffer. The first years of his life were ones of constant political struggle, uncertainty, and persecution, during which his father was in and out of prison for his faith in Christ. All of his seventy-four years were ones of overcoming great difficulties. Watts was chronically ill throughout much of his adult life, suffering with a continual low-grade fever and often enduring intense physical discomfort.

Moreover, Watts lived with inescapable personal unattractiveness. Put bluntly, he was not a handsome man. This is big for Americans, who spend $15 billion a year on cosmetic surgery—one hundred times the entire annual gross domestic product of Uganda. We might dismiss the significance of his ugliness by assuming his society did not care about such frivolities. But it did.

Perhaps next only to our own, people in the Enlightenment were profoundly preoccupied with physical appearance and adornment, including ridiculously elaborate wigs, male make-up, and pink satin culottes—for men. In our therapeutic culture, Watts would be a candidate for insecurity and a life of low self-esteem. Today his doctor would prescribe counseling, perhaps a regimen of anti-depressant drugs—and a face-lift.

Furthermore, Watts held religious views that were the mockery of the elite in his society, and he made the unforgiveable social blunder of not attending the right schools. As a nonconformist, he was unwelcomed at Oxford and Cambridge, and was forced to attend small, insignificant institutions, under the censure and scorn of a refined society.

We need Watts for many reasons. We need his poetry to aid us in recovering a sanctified understanding and imagination. We need him to help reform worship and singing in our churches today. And all of us who have ever felt marginalized for our frailty, our unattractiveness, our lack of formal learning in elite schools, or for any other limitation—real or perceived—need Watts. All people will find a wealth of enrichment and encouragement by learning more of the poetic wonder of Isaac Watts.

CHEATED BY RAW EMOTION

As the Church flounders about in the "liturgical fidget," as C. S. Lewis called it, Isaac Watts (and many other luminaries of Church history and hymnody) can give us both the theological and liturgical ballast Christian worship so desperately needs. And he can give us an emotional rudder, a means of steering the passions in worship by objective propositional truth feelingly delivered. Without such a rudder, worship is shipwrecked on the shoals of cheap-trick emotionalism generated in much the same way it is at a rock concert or a football game. Tragically, in place of singing psalms, hymns, and spiritual songs in worship to Jesus Christ (Colossians 1:16–17), raw feelings of having done so may be supplanting the real thing.

Watts was around nearly three hundred years before Little Richard said, "The blues had an illegitimate baby and we named it rock and roll." But he understood important things about how human beings are wired,

174

things Little Richard and his offspring understand, but which are suppressed or ignored by many Christians today. Watts understood that "our passions are intensely directed toward material things but are hardly moved by the most important discoveries of faith." Warring against the stale lifeless singing in worship in his youth, Watts rightly wanted to see emotion and passion, as we do, in sung worship. He knew that passions "are glorious and noble instruments of the spiritual life when under good conduct."

MISCHIEVOUS ENERGIES

But here is where Watts is a counter voice to many well-meaning worship leaders today; he knew that passions "are ungovernable and mischievous energies when they go astray." He grasped—and so must we—that it is the business of church leaders both "to assist the devout emotions" and "to guard against the abuse of them." Centuries before the invention of the electric bass, Watts warned church leaders: "Let him not begin with their emotions. He must not artfully manipulate" their passions and feelings until he has first "set these doctrines before the eye of their understanding and reasoning faculties. The emotions are neither the guides to truth nor the judges of it." He argued that since "light comes before heat . . . Christians are best prepared for the useful and pious exercise of their emotions in the spiritual life who have laid the foundations in an ordered knowledge of the things of God," foundations that are not being remarkably laid in any ordered fashion in many churches today.

FIRST LIGHT THEN HEAT

In the very best of Watts' hymns, he combines both emotion and knowledge. But for Watts, it is always light first, then heat. The feeling of wonder, the emotion of profound gratitude, the escalating thrill of adoration and praise always follow the objective propositional exploration of the doctrines of the gospel. For Watts, the doxological always followed the theological. And the foundation of ordered knowledge of the things of God that must precede true doxology is essential for all Christians, men and women, rich and poor, in all times and in all places, those with PhDs or GEDs, men from every tribe, kindred, people, and language. We know this not because Watts said so. Watts discovered it from divine revelation. Hebrew poetry in the Bible can be deeply passionate, even erotic, and the psalms are rich with thrilling emotion, but it is always light first, then heat. Surely this is what the apostle Paul was getting at when he wrote, "I will sing praise with my spirit, but I will sing with my mind also" (1 Cor. 14:15b).

FEAST OF DEVOTION

The best way to discover this, however, is not by reading Watts' prose arguments. Read and sing his hymns. A generation of Christians that returns to Watts' feast of devotion spread before us in his hymns will find celebratory nourishment for both mind and spirit. Watts' grasp of doctrinal truth about Christ and the atonement will become our grasp. His determination to take every thought captive to Christ will become our determination. His love for children and the poor will become our love. His passion for the lost will become our passion. His thrill at the forgiveness of sins will become our thrill. His praise will become our praise. His awe will become our awe. His wonder at Christ's saving love for sinners will become our wonder.

All who long for Christ, for being like him, for adoring him, for serving him, for sharing his grace with the world, will find in Watts a treasure trove of experiential doctrine, richly adorning biblical truth that leads to the most thrilling passion for Christ.

CHEAT OF DEVOTION

What about a Christian culture that abandons Watts? We should expect to continue to be cheated by raw emotion masquerading as spiritual light. I for one do not want for an instant to be thrilled with emotion, to become a junkie of my feelings, to be enslaved to raw passion—and tell myself it's Christ with which I'm thrilled. I don't want a cheat. I want Christ. I want to examine from every angle the wondrous cross on which my Savior willingly gave up his perfect life for my miserable, unworthy one. I want to see his head, his hands, his feet, the blood and water of his sorrow and love flow mingling down, washing me clean from my guilt and corruption. I want to survey with wonder a love so amazing and so divine. Then, and only then, I want to be carried away, dazzled beyond words, with Jesus my atoning sacrifice, my gracious substitute, my perfect righteousness.

By the gracious gifting of Jesus, Watts was given a gift of timeless poetic wonder. It was a unique genius. We cannot have it; it was Watts' gift. But it was a gift given first for the glory of God and then for the edification of the Church until we reach that "land of pure delight." By it, every generation of God's children can take Watts' words as their own. By his poetic devotion, every Christian can share in his wonder at Christ and the glories of the world to come.

When I survey the wondrous cross
On which the Prince of glory died,
My richest gain I count but loss,
And pour contempt on all my pride.

Forbid it, Lord, that I should boast,
Save in the death of Christ my God:
All the vain things that charm me most,
I sacrifice them to his blood.

See, from his head, his hands, his feet,
Sorrow and love flow mingled down:
Did e'er such love and sorrow meet,
Or thorns compose so rich a crown?

Were the whole realm of nature mine,
That were a present far too small;
Love so amazing, so divine,
Demands my soul, my life, my all.

12

WHAT MAKES A GREAT HYMN

R eally good hymns are exceedingly rare," wrote J. C. Ryle. "There are only a few men in any age who can write them." For Ryle, Augustus Toplady was one of those few. But in a post-poetry age, how are we to develop the discernment to identify what makes a hymn a great hymn? What qualities make a hymn capture the spiritual imagination of generations of Christians? The question posed another way, what qualities make a hymn writer able to craft such a hymn?

One hymnologist gives an evocative description of the sweat and blood that goes into penning the finest hymns. The poet is not first and foremost concerned with niceties of style, and witty turns of phrase. Caught up with devotional fervor, the hymn writer is compared with Bunyan's Pilgrim in mortal combat with the fiend:

The writer seeks to express his devotional fever, and succeeds [when, he, like] Christian is in deadly strife with Apollyon, when darts fly thick, and the ground is slippery with scales, blood and spume, his chief thought is not whether the coat on his back is of the latest cut from Paris. Indeed, he is so busy with his adversary that he does not know whether he has a coat or a back either. In a quieter moment he can polish his stanza, that is if his stanza admits of polish; but he will in no case sacrifice his original meaning, or weaken even so little as a single line, just for the purpose of tickling the foolish ear of the peddler or the dilettante.

Though it is impossible to know precisely whether Toplady experienced this kind of violent "blood and spume" as he wrote "Rock of Ages," there are clear evidences in the hymn itself of the unction and brilliance that must have animated its author when he wrote it.

ROCK OF AGES

"The most popular hymn in the English language," wrote hymnologist Francis Arthur Jones in 1903 of Toplady's "Rock of Ages." But as with popular things they sometimes get tampered with. There is a persistent, though highly unlikely, story behind the writing of this hymn. The story appeared in the *London Times* in the late 19th century in an account given by Sir William Henry Wills, landowner in Blagdon:

Toplady was one day overtaken by a heavy thunderstorm in Burrington Coombe, on the edge of my property (Blagdon), a rocky glen running up into the heart of the Mendip range, and there, taking shelter between two massive pillars of our native limestone, he penned the hymn, "Rock of Ages, Cleft for Me."

This often-repeated story has been ornamented and expanded to include Toplady casting about for something on which to write the lines as they came to him. Finding no paper in his pockets, he resorted to scouring the dirt floor of the cleft into which he had hidden himself for shelter. The manufacturers of hymn stories could not pass up the ironies: Toplady discovered at his feet a playing card apparently dropped by a previous—and more vulgar—shelterer in the cleft. The tale has him hastily write down the hymn on the card. One skeptic insists that there are a number of American libraries and museums who have on display the original playing card with Toplady's first draft written on it, suggesting rather strongly that it is the American love of sentimentality and sensationalism that fuels such hymnological fabrications.

What is known to be true is that in 1775, twelve years after the episode when Toplady took refuge from a storm in the crags of Burrington Coombe, and just three years before his death, Toplady's famous hymn was first published in the *Gospel Magazine*, and reprinted the next year in a collection of hymns compiled by Toplady.

HOLIEST BELIEVER IN THE WORLD

Hymn XXIII in Toplady's *Psalms and Hymns* bears the heading, "A living and dying prayer for the holiest believer in the world." We might blanch when we first read the title Toplady gave the hymn. Is he referring to himself as the "holiest believer in the world"? Doesn't that seem a bit arrogant? Or is this a shot at his contemporary John

Wesley, a thumbing-the-nose at Wesley's perfectionism? But when we connect the title with the theological substance undergirding the poetry, misunderstanding dissolves.

Toplady, who often wrote, "I am worse than nothing for I am a vile sinner," could not have been preening his own righteousness here. But in one sense it was a jab at Wesley's perfectionism. "Nothing in my hands I bring," wrote Toplady. "Simply to thy cross I cling," Here is seen the eminently practical character of Toplady's Calvinism. It was Christ's imputed righteousness alone that made him the "holiest believer in the world," and nothing else. Clearly it was the alien righteousness of Jesus to which Toplady referred in the title, and, as he had argued with Wesley, his own imagined righteousness is filthy rags in God's sight. And for Toplady what was true in justification was equally true in sanctification.

Ironically, the doctrine of imputed righteousness is adorned in a near perfect poetic conjunction by both Toplady and Wesley. The year Toplady was born, 1740, Wesley translated and versified a marvelous hymn of Ludwig von Zinzendorf's, "Jesus, They Blood and Righteousness." In that hymn I can't imagine a single phrase that expresses a theology with which Toplady would not have wholeheartedly agreed. When crafting a hymn to sing in worship, Wesley seemed compelled to lay aside his syncretism. On the resurrection day, when standing before the glory of God in heaven, Wesley wrote, "This shall be all my plea, Jesus hath lived, hath died for me," perfectly expressing the Calvinist doctrine of the active and passive obedience of Christ for sinners.

NATIONAL DEBT AND GRACE

A satirical essay Toplady wrote in 1775 not only gives us insight into his wit and into the mounting taxation crisis in the American colonies, but it provides us with perspective on his most enduring hymn. Toplady entitled the essay "Questions and answers relative to the National Debt." Royal squandering and the debilitating price tag and territorial losses of The Seven Years' War (1754–1763) had left Britain teetering on financial disaster. The national debt was headline news, as anyone living in today's world can appreciate.

Just as economists attempt to help us get our minds around the quantity of 100-dollar bills it takes to make a trillion dollars, Toplady attempted to help readers visualize just how vast England's debt was by describing how long it would take a man counting 100 shillings an hour to count the debt. If he did nothing else but count shillings throughout his life, the counter would have to live ninety-eight years, 316 days, fourteen hours and forty minutes—and no stopping to eat or sleep.

Toplady was just getting warmed up. He went on to calculate the weight of a shilling and then what 2,600,000,000 shillings weighed. Then he calculated how much weight an oxcart could carry and concluded it would require 20,968 carts to transport the debt. Next he figured out how far two-and-a-half billion shillings would stretch around the globe if laid side by side, and then how much interest it cost England to maintain such enormous debt. He finally concluded there wasn't enough money in all Europe to pay off the debt. Some things never change.

But Toplady was not merely engaged in a witty exercise in economic and political satire. The enormity of the national debt, for Toplady, provided an elaborate metaphor for explaining the gospel of grace. Just as it was impossible for England to pay her financial debt, Toplady proceeded to show how impossible it is for us to pay our sin debt to God. He calculated how great the debt of sin owed to God is if a person sinned once in twenty-four hours, twice in a day, once an hour, once a minute, and finally once every second. He estimated that if a man lived eighty years (Toplady would live only thirty-eight years) and committed one sin per second, a person would be indebted to God for a total of 2,522,880,000 sins. Toplady concluded that each of us is hopelessly lost because of our enormous debt of sin—lost beyond recovery and destined to pay our own debt for all eternity in hell.

UNSHAKEABLE FOUNDATION

Following on the reasoning in his essay on debt, Toplady published "Rock of Ages" in 1776 in a collection of sacred poetry entitled *Psalms and Hymns*. Intensely personal and filled with evocative imagery, little could Toplady have known that it would become one of the greatest hymns in the English language:

Rock of Ages, cleft for me
Let me hide myself in thee;
Let the water and the blood,
From thy riven side which flowed,
Be of sin the double cure
Cleanse me from its guilt and power.

Toplady may have drawn the language of the hymn from Isaiah 26:4 where the coming Messiah is referred to as the "everlasting Rock." He would have been conversant with other biblical imagery of this kind: God gave Israel water in the wilderness when Moses struck a rock; God hid Moses in the cleft of a rock when God's glory passed by; later, the Apostle Paul explains that Christ is the spiritual Rock, the firm foundation and the only refuge for lost sinners.

> Not the labour of my hands
> Can fulfill thy law's demands;
> Could my zeal no respite know,
> Could my tears forever flow,
> All for sin could not atone;
> Thou must save, and thou alone.

In one of his polemic works, Toplady had ably argued that Wesley's Arminianism and perfectionism led inexorably back to the works righteousness taught by the Roman Catholic Church. With Pauline clarity and psalm-like skill, Toplady adorned the doctrine of man's total inability to meet the perfect requirement of God's holy law: "Not the labor of my hands /Can fulfill thy law's demands." No amount of well-intentioned zeal, no endlessly-flowing tears of regret could save the sinner: "Thou must save, and thou alone." Toplady would be the first to admit that there was nothing theologically innovative here, though there is masterful poetic originality in how he expressed these timeless truths of the gospel.

> Nothing in my hand I bring,
> Simply to thy cross I cling;

Naked, come to thee for dress;
Helpless, look to thee for grace;
Foul, I to the Fountain fly;
Wash me, Saviour, or I die.

Just as in his preaching Toplady kept Christ and his cross at the center of his message, so in his poetry he held high the cross of the Savior. Nothing else would do to satisfy the enormous debt the sinner owes.

While I draw this fleeting breath,
When mine eyelids close in death,
When I soar to worlds unknown,
See thee on thy judgment throne,
Rock of Ages, cleft for me,
Let me hide myself in thee.

Penned by a pastor who preached as a "dying man to dying men," here Toplady adorns the sinner's hope when facing death and soaring "to worlds unknown." When the sinner stands before the judgment bar of God, he won't look to "the labors of [his] hands," or to his all-too-pathetic faithfulness, or to his partial obedience. He will hide himself in the atoning sacrifice and perfect righteousness of Jesus Christ alone. Because our sins are so great, there is absolutely nothing we can do to fulfill God's holy demands. But God sent his beloved Son to do for us what we could not do for ourselves.

INFLUENCE OF ROCK OF AGES

It has been said that "No other English hymn can be named which has laid so broad and firm a grasp upon the

English-speaking world" as Toplady's "Rock of Ages." An illustration of this occurred early in 1892, as Albert Victor, grandson of Queen Victoria, lay dying of influenza. It is told that he recited "Rock of Ages, Cleft for me" on his deathbed. "For if in this hour," he reportedly said, "I had only my worldly honors and dignities to depend upon, I should be poor indeed."

Hymnologist W. T. Stead in his volume *Hymns That Have Helped* records that when the steamer *London* went down in the Bay of Biscay, January 11, 1866, the last boatload of people rescued from the ship said they heard the doomed passengers singing "Rock of Ages" as they went down with the ship.

Another revealing story about the hymn is told of a 19th century missionary in India eager to spread the good news of the gospel of free grace to the predominantly Hindu population. Certain that "Rock of Ages, Cleft for me," would provide imagery the native population could grasp, the zealous missionary hired a native Hindu student to translate Toplady's hymn into Sanskrit. When the work was completed, the missionary eagerly translated the Hindu student's version back into English to see how the hymn had fared in the translation. Imagine his disappointment when he read the opening lines:

Very old stone, split for my benefit,
Let me absent myself
under one of your fragments.

Perhaps this is what poet, physician Elliot Emanuel meant when he observed that "poetry is what eludes translation." The young missionary discovered that though original truths may be translated, the imagery and subtle nuances of language are entirely another matter.

Ironically, Toplady's "Rock of Ages" even made its way into Wesleyan hymnals, but usually with the poet's name "regulated to decent obscurity in out-of-the-way indexes," as Bernard L. Manning puts it. This practice, alas, served to confuse the authorship of some hymns. Many Methodists and critics of Toplady still maintain that Toplady plagiarized "Rock of Ages" from their founder, John Wesley, though I can find nothing more than envious partisanship to support this claim; it may have been motivated solely as tit-for-tat at Toplady who several times exposed Wesley's plagiarism.

Another evidence of the enduring nature of Toplady's finest hymn takes place weekly in his hometown. While leading one of my Church history tours, the organist at St. Andrews Parish Church, Farnham, where Toplady was baptized, told us that they honor one of their greatest sons by concluding every evening worship service by singing a stanza from "Rock of Ages."

EXTRAVAGANT PRAISE

Lamenting that Toplady did not live longer, write more hymns and engage in fewer controversies, J. C. Ryle, nevertheless, ranks Toplady as one of the greatest of English hymn writers:

> I give it as my decided opinion that he was one of the best hymn writers in the English language. I am quite aware that this may seem extravagant praise; but I speak deliberately. I hold that there are no hymns better than his.

Ryle, the great evangelical Anglican bishop of the 19th century, proceeds to explain more precisely his reasons for saying this.

Of all the English hymn writers, none perhaps, have succeeded so thoroughly in combining truth, poetry, life, warmth, fire, solemnity, and unction as Toplady has.

"Truth, poetry, life, warmth, fire, solemnity, and unction." Perhaps in these words Ryle has given us one of the most succinct and precise definitions of what a hymn actually is. Yet as highly as I regard Toplady—and Ryle—is he over-stating his praise of the hymn writer? "Rock of Ages" most certainly is one of the finest English hymns, but most of Toplady's poetic efforts fall short of its richness and pathos. Nevertheless, there are several of his hymns that are very fine and—like Toplady himself—deserve to be better known and loved.

POLEMICS OVER POETRY

Toplady's doctrinal zeal at times had a detrimental effect on his poetry. I wonder, reading some of his poetry—poetry I have never sung or seen in any hymnal—if he failed to keep the purpose of poetry before his mind as he wrote. The strength and sphere of poetry is more for adorning truth—what Toplady does so magnificently in "Rock of Ages"—than declaring or propounding it. I'm reminded of the self-criticism of Unitarian poet and literary critic James Russell Lowell (1819–1891) who wrote of his own poetic limitations:

The top of the hill he will ne'er come nigh reaching
Till he learns the distinction 'twixt singing and
preaching.

In lines from his "Hymn of Sovereign Grace,"
Toplady seems to suffer from the same limitation. True
as his words are, one feels more the thunder of the
polemicist than the passion of the penitent in the
declarative lines:

Thy Spirit does not offer life,
But raises from the dead;
And neither asks the sinner's leave,
Nor needs the sinner's aid.

This is more a thesis-argument poem, a versified
essay, than a hymn. If Ryle tended to overstate his praise
of Toplady, hymnologist Erik Routley (1917–1982)
unfairly disparages his poetic gift. "Toplady could write,"
he said, "that is to say, he could write prose, for he was no
poet," Measured by the above quatrain alone, Routley
might be able to defend his statement.

In another stanza, Toplady seems again to be more
the polemicist than the poet, yet he captures in a few
succinct lines the truth that good works do not save us,
nor do they keep us saved. Good works are the fruit of
God's sovereign power first renewing the tree:

Thy power, before the fruit is good,
Must first renew the tree;
We rise, and work the works of God,

When wrought upon by thee.

This is good theology, but not great hymn poetry. Though it imbeds right theology in verse, it lacks the impassioned grace necessary to awaken the heart and imagination of the worshiper to the high praise of God. I suspect Toplady felt rather good about the salvo delivered from the metrical cannon of these lines. I equally suspect that, since he wrote these lines, they have only rarely found their way into the singing of Christian worship. The tone and syntax lend more to preaching than singing. The best hymns adorn the doctrinal truths of the gospel with passion, skill, and grateful adoration. And Toplady on a few occasions did just that.

DEBTOR TO MERCY ALONE

We can always count on Toplady to get the gospel right; that is without argument. In a hymn written in 1771, Toplady not only got the gospel right, but he achieved more of that passionate adorning quality so essential to a great hymn.

A debtor to mercy alone,
Of covenant mercy I sing;
Nor fear, with thy righteousness on,
My person and offering to bring.

The terrors of law and of God
With me can have nothing to do;
My Savior's obedience and blood
Hide all my transgressions from view.

Toplady is not here the determined polemicist, parrying the thrust of his Arminian attackers. He is the trembling, awe-struck Christian, on his face in gratitude for the imputed righteousness of Jesus applied to his unworthy life.

> The work which his goodness began
> The arm of his strength will complete;
> his promise is yea and amen,
> And never was forfeited yet.

> Things future, nor things that are now,
> Not all things below nor above
> Can make him his purpose forego,
> Or sever my soul from his love.

Though not his finest lines of poetry, yet here Toplady turns the forgiven sinner away from himself and to the promises of the gospel, to the Heavenly Father who began a good work in redeemed sinners and, as promised, will perform it until the day of Jesus Christ (Philippians 1:6). For Toplady it is God's arm of strength that is the basis of Christian assurance, not our performance. God never reneges on his promises; hence the frailest Christian is assured because he is hidden in Christ. The saints in heaven may be more happy now than chronically ill Toplady was when he penned these indelible lines, but they are not more secure than any Christian is in the present, hidden as we are in the cleft of Jesus' blood and righteousness.

> My name from the palms of his hands

Eternity will not erase;
Impressed on his heart it remains
In marks of indelible grace.

Yes, I to the end shall endure,
As sure as the earnest is given.
More happy, but not more secure,
The glorified spirits in heaven.

There is an intimate, personal quality to these lines, and though they portray Toplady's own heart and experience of grace, they encompass a universal application that extends to all worshiping Christians. What confidence does the timorous Christian gain when taking Toplady's words on his own lips! Do any more thrilling words of assurance exist in the canon of Christian hymns?

More happy, but not more secure,
The glorified spirits in heaven.

"But not more secure." And why not more secure? Toplady understood that because of the imputed righteousness of Christ, the Christian is righteous before God now. Though we grow in grace, though we are being sanctified, "the work of God's free grace" in us, our righteous standing before God, secured by the active obedience of Christ our righteousness, makes our standing with God absolutely secure. Yes, we certainly do look forward to glorification in heaven, but we will not be more secure in heaven than we are right now in

193

Christ. Such is the soul-comforting theology Toplady celebrates in this hymn.

Reformed University Fellowship campus pastor Kevin Twit borrowed the name of his music ministry from the fourth line of Toplady's final stanza, "indelible grace." Kevin discovered the hymn while scouring C. H. Spurgeon's *Our Own Hymnbook* for biblically rich lyrics, accessible to university students at Belmont University, Nashville, Tennessee. When he discovered Toplady, he knew he had found what he was searching for. Indelible grace, for Toplady, is grace that no created thing can erase, grace that is impossible to remove or rub out, grace that is indelible, that remains forever.

It sounds redundant: grace that really is grace. Can there be any other kind of grace? But because we proud sinners are constantly tampering with the gospel, redefining grace to include just a little bit of our obedience or our faithfulness, every generation is forced to employ adjectives and superlatives to get it into our stubborn hide that salvation is entirely the free, unmerited gift of a stupendously merciful God.

HOW VAST THE BENEFITS DIVINE

In another hymn of Toplady that deserves more often to be sung by the Church, he seemed to anticipate how theological revisionists would be introducing "false and corrupt opinions," attempting to make sanctification a condition of justification today. Did he have a premonition that there would be yet future generations within the Church who would be suspicious that preaching free grace will lead to Antinomianism, men who are fearful that proclaiming the good news that

Jesus, indeed, paid it all, and all to him we owe, that such a message would undermine morality and good works?

How vast the benefits divine
Which we in Christ possess!
We are redeemed from guilt and shame
And called to holiness.

But not for works which we have done,
Or shall hereafter do,
Hath God decreed on sinful men
Salvation to bestow.

The Father's saving purpose in Christ had nothing to do with our fitness before regeneration or our fitness after. Toplady did indeed understand that we have been chosen for holiness, but he never lost his grip on the fact that it is God who is at work in his elect to accomplish what he promises, both in justification and sanctification. Toplady understood that only when salvation is by grace alone, through faith alone, in Christ alone, would God receive all the glory alone.

The glory, Lord, from first to last,
Is due to thee alone;
Aught to ourselves we dare not take,
Or rob thee of thy crown.

Our glorious Surety undertook
To satisfy for man,
And grace was given us in him
Before the world began.

Certainly, Toplady is on solid theological ground here, though perhaps not soaring on the highest plane of poetic imagery. Nevertheless, there are few hymns that achieve the degree of soteriological clarity coupled with poetry as this hymn.

This is thy will, that in thy love
We ever should abide;
That earth and hell should not prevail
To turn thy Word aside.

Not one of all the chosen race
But shall to Heav'n attain,
Partake on earth the purposed grace
And then with Jesus reign.

One need only read Wesley on free will and conditional justification to understand why Toplady felt compelled to conclude this hymn with soaring Pauline confidence. Equally one need only read Paul in Romans 8, "There is therefore now no condemnation for those who are in Christ Jesus... What can separate us from the love of God which is in Christ Jesus?" Not earth nor hell. When he is for us who can be against us? Purposed grace for Toplady meant that grace by its very definition is certain, purposed in God's eternal, merciful decree "that in thy love we ever should abide." Or as Toplady's contemporary Philip Doddridge expressed it so beautifully:

Grace, 'tis a charming sound,

Harmonious to mine ear;
Heaven with the echo shall resound,
And all the earth shall hear.

13

WORSHIP AND IDOLATRY

Co-founder and lead singer of the Grunge band Nirvana, Kurt Cobain may have been clueless that he was screaming the anthem of an entire generation in his 1991 hit "Smells Like Teen Spirit."

> With the lights out it's less dangerous;
> Here we are now entertain us.
> I feel stupid and contagious;
> Here we are now entertain us.

Cobain and many pop musical entertainers like him became the idols of a youth culture that wanted what they were delivering, entertainment. But, tragically, it was not only the teen spirit of the unbelieving world that joined in the mantra "entertain us."

Christians in the contemporary church have been stumbling over themselves to catch up with the world. The transformation is nearly complete. The options before us are to sing hymns with "biblically rich content," as Keith Getty wrote, or to continue "entertaining teenagers with something that will not hold water when they hit college or head out into the workplace." Getty contrasts singing that is "credible and powerful" with what is merely "cultural and optional."

Alas, on the whole, we have refashioned what we do in worship to look far more like what is pop-cultural and disposable, far more like teen-culture entertainment on the stage at a Nirvana concert, necessary changes constantly being revised to match the vicissitudes of each iteration of the latest thing since 1991.

IDOL FACTORIES

"…every one of us is, even from his mother's womb," wrote John Calvin, "a master craftsman of idols." Calvin and the Reformers of the 16th century knew something that we have almost entirely ignored today. Left to ourselves, we will create idols out of almost anything, including those who entertain us. Intractable rebels against God, we cast about to find something else to venerate, to bow down to, to worship. But when we Christians do it, we desperately keep trying to tell ourselves that we're not doing it, that it's still all about Jesus.

Nowhere was this more obvious than in medieval worship in the Roman Catholic Church. Of course, the RCC continued to talk about Jesus, his deity, his virgin birth, his bodily resurrection, but over the centuries they had added rivals. Layers of sacraments, including bowing down and praying to images of saints and Mary, lighting candles to them, going on pilgrimages to venerate their relics—all of these and more had supplanted the true worship of God. And Calvin took these perversions seriously because he believed "...there is nothing more perilous to our salvation than a preposterous and perverse worship of God."

Enter a medieval church in Calvin's day (or today) and one could not help seeing the priorities of medieval worship. Front and center, gold-gilded, demanding the full attention of worshipers, was the altar on which the priest transubstantiated the bread and wine into the body and blood of Christ; the central act of Roman Catholic worship was on full display for all to see.

Pause and reflect with me on what an outside observer would conclude about the priorities of contemporary worship. What is front and center, on full display, glittering on the stage, demanding the sole attention of worshipers? All the paraphernalia of entertainment worship: cords, gadgets, glittering instruments, drum set encased in plexiglass, microphones, emotive lighting, and an array of performers stretching across the stage.

Deeply troubled by the "perverse worship of God" in their day, the Reformers set about returning to the Bible alone, wherein they discovered that we are justified by grace alone, through faith alone, in Christ alone, to the glory of God alone. This rediscovery of the gospel of grace led to a robust biblical theology about salvation and the gospel. Concurrent with the reformation of theology was a reformation of doxology, of how we enter into the presence of the living God in worship.

Knox, Calvin, and the Reformers proceeded to help break the chains of the idolatrous medieval corruptions that had been allowed to infect every dimension of corporate worship. Because "The mind of man is like a work place of idolatry," as Calvin put it, they scoured the Scriptures to learn what worship pleases God.

THE REGULATIVE PRINCIPLE

From their labors came what theologians call the Regulative Principle of Worship. I'd like to demonstrate that everybody in the worship wars has a regulative principle, that is, some controlling idea behind the choices that are made about what we do in church, how we order our service, the place and role of the sacraments, how and what we pray, read, preach, and sing. These components of worship never emerge out of thin air. We do them, or don't do them, based on what is regulating our understanding.

Everybody has a regulative principle. Some churches regulate their worship by the past, tradition, and how they've always done things. There may have been more foundation in generations past, but for all intents and purposes today, they do what they do, how they do it, because that's just how they've always done it.

Others regulate what they do in worship by their preference. These churches order their service of worship by what people like. What makes them feel good in worship, what gives them a sense of having worshiped when they're finished. People who choose to attend these churches might say, I go to this church because it's what I like and enjoy.

Still other churches organize their gatherings by the pragmatic principle of worship. They do what they do and how they do it because they believe it works. They regulate how they worship by what fills the church, what draws people into the church. For these churches what is popular and entertaining works. It draws people in.

Closely related to the pragmatic principle of worship are those churches that have concluded that they can do anything in church as long as it is not specifically prohibited in the Bible.

The Reformers rejected all of these principles informing worship. They believed that idolatry results from regulating worship by the past, by the pragmatic, by personal preferences, by doing anything not prohibited. Calvin concluded that a prescriptive principle of worship ought to regulate what and how we come into the presence of the living God in worship. Reformed theologians concluded that true worship is commanded worship; we may only include in our worship what God has commanded us to include in his Word.

The Regulative Principle of Worship is summarized in John Knox's emphatic assertion: "All worshiping, honoring, or service, invented by the brain of man in the religion of God, without his own express commandment, is idolatry."

This meant some pretty serious housecleaning for the Reformers. Iconoclasm, the breaking of idols, resulted throughout Scotland and much of Europe as men, zealous for purity of doctrine and of doxology, tore down the idols that cluttered medieval church buildings.

A century later, the Westminster Divines, the leading pastors and theologians of 16th century England and Scotland, encapsulated the Regulative Principle of Worship in the most biblically careful and thorough Reformed confession of faith:

The acceptable way of worshiping the true God is instituted by himself, and so limited by his own revealed will, that he may not be worshiped according to the imaginations and devices of men, or the suggestions of Satan, under any visible representation or any other way not prescribed in the holy Scripture (WCF 21.1).

Put simply, these godly men wanted the Church to worship God's way not the world's way.

PRESCRIPTIVE SINGING

What does the Regulative Principle of Worship tell us about music, about what and how we sing in worship?

For the answer, we will find it instructive to hear practical ways the Reformers employed music in worship. Calvin and Luther agreed about the power of music: "There is scarcely anything in this world which can more turn or bend hither and thither the ways of men. We know by experience that music has a secret and almost incredible power to move hearts." Though Calvin argues against those who wanted to condemn all music, still, this knowledge about the force of music led him to be more cautious than Luther. "Therefore, we ought to be even more diligent in regulating it in such a way that it shall be useful to us and in no way pernicious."

Calvin, who believed that all good things were gifts of God, also knew that, intractable sinners that we are, good gifts can easily become idols. Good things can become god things, as one man put it. Yet, Calvin maintained a high view of the importance of music in worship: "And in truth we know by experience that singing has great force and vigor to move and inflame the hearts of men to invoke and praise God with a more vehement and ardent zeal." Because Calvin knew the "force and vigor" of music, he gives us wisdom on what kind of music is appropriate in the house of God:

> Care must always be taken that the song be neither light nor frivolous; but that it have weight and majesty (as St. Augustine says), and also, there is a great difference between music which one makes to entertain men at table and in their houses, and the psalms which are sung in the Church in the presence of God and his angels.

Calvin understood something about music that we have suppressed in the last generation. Music is not neutral. There are different kinds of music that may be appropriate in various settings, but musical styles are not interchangeable. Not all music is capable of bearing the weight of the majesty of the God into whose presence we are entering to adore. Calvin ranks entertainment music as "light and frivolous" and thereby inappropriate for corporate worship. Only music with "weight and majesty" was appropriate for the worship of the God revealed in Scripture.

Geneva was a party city, a trading center, a crossroads where many merchants, far from home, came and went. He had seen the abuse of music on the streets and in the taverns, music that gave only "…foolish delight by which it seduces men from better employments and occupies them in vanity." Geneva was a Vanity Fair, the Las Vegas of Europe, a culture, like ours, screaming to be entertained, and this atmosphere exerted its pressures on the church, as it does today. Calvin had heard with his own ears the force of music when it was combined with unwholesome lyrics: "When melody goes with [music], every bad word penetrates more deeply into the heart...Just as a funnel conveys the wine into the depths of the decanter, so venom and corruption are distilled into the very bottom of the heart by melody."

MUSIC WITH WEIGHT AND MAJESTY

Above everything, Calvin wanted music and singing in Saint Pierre to exalt the glory of God, and where better to find such songs than in the inspired Psalms of David? In Psalms, Calvin discovered "an anatomy of all the parts of the soul."

Meanwhile, Geneva became the refugee center of Europe, and Calvin soon learned that God had brought several people with particular musical gifts to the city-state. Clement Marot, court poet of France, he put to work versifying the psalms in French, and enlisted musician Louis Bourgeoise to compose melodies with "weight and majesty," but that would also be accessible to common folks worshiping in the church.

While Calvin was in exile from 1538-1541 in hymn-singing Strasbourg, he wrote several treatises, but he never wrote anything against singing hymns of human composition rather than only psalms in corporate worship. An inexplicable omission for Calvin, if he was as vehement as some are about exclusive psalm singing as some insist.

What's more, during his time as pastor of the French-speaking church in Strasbourg, a hymn of human composition appeared entitled, "I greet thee who my sure Redeemer art." Some historians and hymnologists believe it was written by Calvin himself. We may never know this side of eternity, but we do know that when Calvin returned to Geneva, he included this hymn and others in the *Geneva Psalter* 1551, set to *Toulon* a fitting melody composed by Louis Bourgeois.

Imagine Calvin leading his congregation at Saint Pierre in singing this glorious hymn, not only as a call to worship, but as a rehearsal of the whole of the gospel and the life of a Christian whose only hope is in "the King of mercy and of grace."

I greet thee, who my sure Redeemer art,
My only trust and Savior of my heart,
Who pain didst undergo for my poor sake;
I pray thee from our hearts all cares to take.

Thou art the King of mercy and of grace,
Reigning omnipotent in every place;
So come, O King, and our whole being sway;
Shine on us with the light of thy pure day.

Calvin knew that if we are to worship aright, we must preserve the pure doctrine of the gospel, and understanding and adoring God's sovereign authority over salvation and all things was non-negotiable, both in life and as we "walk through the valley of the shadow of death."

Thou art the life, by which alone we live,
And all our substance and our strength receive;
O comfort us in death's approaching hour,
Strong-hearted then to face it by thy power.

Thou hast the true and perfect gentleness,
No harshness hast thou and no bitterness;
Make us to taste the sweet grace found in thee
And ever stay in thy sweet unity.

Our hope is in no other save in thee;
Our faith is built upon thy promise free;
O grant to us such stronger hope and sure
That we can boldly conquer and endure.

The God that Calvin adored with all his being, was a God of "true and perfect gentleness," one in whom alone the Christian could "taste the sweet grace," and by whose power and keeping alone be enabled to "boldly conquer and endure."

GRUNTING OF HOGS

We'll never know for sure if Calvin wrote that marvelous hymn, but we know for certain that Luther wrote a number of hymns, including the musical accompaniment. Luther is less guarded and speaks of music with little of the caution Calvin used.

Alongside Calvin, Luther completes our understanding of the role of singing in worship. He laid out his plan: "I wish to compose sacred hymns so that the Word of God may dwell among the people also by means of songs." Setting to work early, Luther published his first congregational hymnbook, *Geystliche Gesangbuchlein*, in 1524. He repudiated the "lazy worship" whereby everything was performed for them and the congregation was passive, observing but not participating in singing. But they needed to learn how to sing together. So, Luther began teaching his people to sing like God sings, with full voice.

Ranking music even higher than Calvin, Luther declared, "Music is an outstanding gift of God and next to theology. I would not give up my slight knowledge of music for a great consideration." He was being overly modest. He played the lute, composed original music, and was called "The nightingale of Wittenberg" for his skillful singing ability. So important was music, Luther was an advocate of formal musical education in the school curriculum for all German children.

Typical of Luther's Teutonic bluntness, he had little good to say about someone who disliked fine music. "A person who does not regard music as a marvelous creation of God, must be a clodhopper indeed and does not deserve to be called a human being; he should be permitted to hear nothing but the braying of asses and the grunting of hogs."

Of Luther's thirty-six hymns, "A Mighty Fortress" is by far and away his best loved. Written likely while he was sequestered in Coburg Castle during the Diet of Augsburg, it is a rousing hymn loosely drawn from Psalm 46, wherein Luther defies "the prince of darkness grim," and declares his allegiance to Christ Jesus, the "right man on our side." Though Christ's name doesn't appear in Psalm 46, Luther was theologically correct to name Christ Jesus in this sturdy battle hymn:

Did we in our own strength confide,
Our striving would be losing,
Were not the right man on our side,
The man of God's own choosing.
Dost ask who that may be?
Christ Jesus, it is he;
Lord Sabaoth his name,
From age to age the same,
And he must win the battle.

Jesus Christ and his gospel regulate what and how we sing in worship, and he is the same yesterday, today, and forever, or as Luther put it, "From age to age the same." It is inimical to the timeless, enduring truth of justification by faith alone to recast it with music that is fashionable—but only for the moment. The trendy trivializes the eternal. In the warfare for true biblical worship, Jesus Christ "must win the battle."

14

GONE AWAY HYMNAL

A dear pastor friend of mine, lamenting the loss of hymnals in so many churches, refers to lyrics projected up on a screen as "off-the-wall songs." He's not a fan. But the popular trend is definitely against him. Most churches see it as a giant step forward to leave their hymnals moldering in the basement of the church, relics of a bygone era, and good riddance.

The rationale is that people are looking up, not fumbling with the pages of an old book. And what about the visitors, unbelievers that come to church? It's way easier for them to just look at the words up on the screen. No hunting for the right page number. No confusing musical score to distract them. It's huge progress to leave those hymnals behind us.

Still more, it is argued that the old hymnal doesn't include all the cool new songs. We're stuck singing lyrics written hundreds of years ago by a bunch of old dead guys. Ewww. The new way lets us add new songs any time we want. Just get the lyrics to the tech guys; they can plunk them into power point slides, and we can sing the latest new thing next week.

NO GATEKEEPERS

But what have we lost by giving up our hymnals? We surrendered scrutiny. Publishing a hymnal is an enormous task, requiring careful organizing of the hymns by themes and biblical texts, also requiring an editorial committee of people chosen because of their literary and theological training and experience. Hymnal editors spent years compiling the best hymns for congregations to sing.

Giving up our hymnals takes all that scrutiny away and leaves us at the mercy of the latest new songs. We need more scruples about the new material. It's way too easy to fabricate a worship song and introduce it next Sunday; no vetting, no scrutiny, no gatekeepers, no hymnal editors.

When we abandoned our hymnals we also abandoned literary and theological standards of orthodoxy and excellence. All too often, emotional nonsense, however well-intentioned, supplants a timeless hymn like Bernard of Clairvaux's "O Sacred Head, Now Wounded" that every Christian needs to sing in corporate worship several times a year and in family worship at least as often. Instead, we endure the singing of vacuous, repetitive lyrics that fall far beneath what is appropriate and well-pleasing to God—the kind of lyrics that used to be in our hymnals because they had undergone the rigor of the centuries.

Without that rigorous scrutiny we may find ourselves joining in a catchy Disneyland song about the world singing God's love, "and we'll all join hands,/every woman, every man,/we'll sing His love." This sounds like it was penned by a universalist Unitarian worship leader. True, every knee will bow and every tongue confess that Jesus is Lord to the glory of God, but unbelievers won't be joining hands and singing his love. They will be weeping and wailing and gnashing their teeth at his wrath.

The hymnal helped us learn our theology, get it not only into our heads but into our hearts. The off-the-wall-song phenomenon hastens theological decline and illiteracy, leaving us vulnerable not only to doxological drivel but to blatant doctrinal error and apostacy.

GONE AWAY BIBLE

Another yet more pernicious loss when we abandoned our hymnals for the power point projection screen, is that in doing so we abandoned our Bibles. When we have the screen up there already, and the tech guys have the power point program at their fingertips, it's simple to project the biblical text up on the screen too. Consequently, few people bring their Bibles to church anymore. Why bother? I realize that this too is motivated by good intentions, even gospel intentions; we want visitors who are unfamiliar with a Bible to see the biblical text under consideration effortlessly, without the distraction of an actual Bible in hand.

Getting your Bible off the screen instead of from, well, the Bible, is the equivalent of taking a nutrition pill instead of pulling your chair up to the dining table and feasting on a slab of grass-fed beef steak with all the delectable accoutrements.

An unintended consequence of getting our Bible from a screen, is that many do not know how to find their way around their Bibles (many can't even find where they last laid their physical copy of the Bible; it's got to be here somewhere). I wonder how many millennials could even find Zephaniah 3:17, back there in the clean pages, in a physical Bible, with pages, margins, a concordance, maps—you know—a real book.

I began annotating the margins of my Bible(s) in college, cross referencing, adding hymn lyrics on similar themes, quotations from Puritans and Reformers, and other great preachers since. My Bible is precious to me. First and last, because it is the Word of God, but also, because I own it. It is the same copy of it I read over and over. It has my marginalia in it. I can reread passages that I read and dated in times of celebration and thanksgiving, and in times of grief and sorrow.

Forfeiting our hymnals in favor of an ephemeral projection screen is one of the greatest contributors to biblical illiteracy. We are no longer a generation of Bible Christians. Oh, sure, we have the app on our phones, with all the notifications popping up to distract us, but we don't truly own our Bibles.

The loss of the Bible leaves us vulnerable to the theology of the new social revolutionaries, shouting their unflinching doctrinal priorities in our faces. One of the ways we can tell when we are being more shaped by our culture than being shapers of it, is when the Bible's language and themes begin to sound odd to our ears, when we feel like we need to make apologies for the biblical authors, worse yet, for the Holy Spirit. They didn't really mean to put it that way. Couldn't they have been more sensitive to the priorities of our culture?

This is yet another important reason the Church must continue singing the psalms and the best hymns of our spiritual forebears. Then, after our minds, hearts, and imaginations have been thoroughly shaped by biblical and historical doxology, only then are we equipped to contribute new appropriate hymns for this generation of Christ's body to sing.

HYMNS AS POETRY

In the course of my research, writing, and teaching about hymns over the last decades I have learned many wonderful things about hymns, hymn writers, and hymnody—and every time I open the hymnal (usually the Trinity) I learn something new.

I love singing hymns. I love the very best of our hymn lyrics from the last 1,800 years or so, and I have come more and more to love them not only as heartfelt passionate expressions of praise to God but as the best of English poetry.

It was American poet John Greenleaf Whittier who said, "The highest use of poetry is the hymn." In addition, I love many of the timeless musical settings of great classic hymn poetry, and I appreciate a growing number of the new hymns that are being written by thoughtful Christian poets and musicians.

Throughout decades of teaching, I have been incorporating the study and imitation of the best hymns as poetry worthy to be studied in its own right in my high school English classes. I have, however, discovered some significant obstacles to understanding and appreciating hymns for this generation of Christian young people.

Nowhere is this more obvious than when students attempt to write about hymns as poetry. I teach my students to explore the meaning of poetry by writing poetry explications, essays written specifically about poetry, wherein they observe and evaluate the effectiveness of the various poetic conventions used and the depth and richness of the meaning.

I've often had my students compare poets with the poetry of hymns written at the same time or in similar circumstances. For example, I include Lutheran pastor Martin Rinkhart's great lyric, "Now Thank We All Our God," written while the Thirty-Years War was raging through Germany, in my course on World War I poets. Rinkhart's 17th century hymn was sung August 1, 1914 on the streets of Berlin when the Kaiser announced the mobilization of German troops to invade Belgium. It makes a dramatic counterpoint to the despair and anger of many of the WW I poets.

STUDENT WRITERS PANIC

Here is where I discovered the obstacle for my students. When I gave them a poem of Wordsworth or Cowper or Shakespeare to analyze and evaluate, they knew what to do. It looked like and read like poetry. It was there in front of them in the format in which the poet originally penned the words. They can observe the basic unit of poetry, the line, with its hard-left margins and capitalized first lines (center lining poetry is a

Hallmark card reduction of meaning and content to visual form and is unlike the format the poet wrote the poetry in). They can find the parallel ideas, the progression of thought, the figures of speech, the allusions, the meter, the rhyme scheme, the poet's use of various sound devices, the use of *inclusio*, and other subtleties of the poetic art. But when I give them a hymn from the *Trinity Hymnal* (one of the best American hymnals; I use it daily), they are frustrated and confused. When I give them a hymn with the poetry imbedded in and subordinated to the musical score, as it appears in almost every American hymnal since the mid-19th century, they panic.

At first, I didn't get this. I grew up singing hymns in church; I read music; I love music. At first, I concluded it was part of the decline of culture, the loss of the ability to read music and sing hymns. But as I traveled to various other countries around the world, I discovered the problem.

Maybe its American exceptionalism again. But I'm not so sure. We Americans seem to be the only ones who hand hymnals to our congregations that have the poetry of the hymns in a subordinate role to the music so it does not look like or read like its genre—poetry. Every other country I have visited (UK, New Zealand, Australia, Tonga, Europe, Japan, Peru, Uganda, etc.) the hymnals have the lyric of the poetry visible as poetry, in lines and stanzas the way the poet wrote it. I have talked to missionaries and Christians from other countries I have not visited. I discovered that we Americans are pretty much the only ones who do this.

REVIVALISM TORPEDOES CONTENT

So, I did some more research. As near as I can find, we began doing this as a direct result of the shift in priorities in 19th century Revivalism. We began replacing many of the psalm versifications from the Reformation, and many of the classic hymns with revival songs that in general were sentimental, repetitive, lacking in theological depth, and addressed largely to the sinner rather than as expressions of worship and adoration to God. This reduction of the content and the quality of lyric went hand in hand with the crafting of new music, designed to attract the lost into the camp meeting tent. The new popular musical sound (the worst of it somewhere between merry-go-round ditty, the frontier cowboy tune, and barbershop quartet sound) became more important because it was the hook to draw in the lost. Music was no longer accompaniment as an aid in taking the meaning of the poetry on the lips and in the heart and mind.

In Protestant Christian worship, music has always been in a subordinate role to aid the worshiper in taking to heart and mind the meaning and richness of the poetic lyric. Though Calvin knew and appreciated the incredible power of music to move hearts, he cautioned against getting music and the objective meaning of the words flipped around, "We must beware lest our ears be more intent on the music than our minds on the spiritual meaning of the words."

In Revivalism, that's precisely what happened, the words became less important. The new format of the hymnal reflects this shifting priority of Revivalism.

Charles Finney's New Measures and Pelagian theology, flipped things around. The new format of the American hymnal, reducing the central importance of the poetry, was born. Open any Revivalism-influenced hymnal and the first thing we see is the musical score not the poetic lines. The format alone does exactly what Calvin cautioned us against, setting us up for our eye and ear to be "more intent on the music than our minds on the spiritual meaning of the words." Music first, the poetry chopped up to fit within the score.

When I gave my English students a timed essay to write under exam conditions about a hymn, I would give them the option of seeing the hymn formatted the way the poet wrote it in lines and stanzas, or formatted with the poetry stripped and dissected to fit the musical format; they chose to have it in poetic form every time. But we might object and say that when we are singing in church we are not writing an essay; they are two entirely different activities.

Though that is true, both activities require the ones reading and singing the poetry to understand the meaning of what they are reading and singing. Christians rightly place a high premium on the engagement of the mind and of the imagination in worship. I would argue that singing hymns from a hymnal inadvertently formatted to make it more difficult to observe the subtleties of the poetry being sung is actually working against its own purpose.

RESCUE THE HYMNAL
Maybe it's time to take on a remaining reductionist influence of Revivalism on our hymnal and thus on our

worship. I propose a cross-page format, the poetry in lines and stanzas on the left, and facing the poetry the musical score. Let's rescue hymn poetry from the influence of Revivalism so that our hymnal format reflects biblical priorities, thereby confronting a significant obstacle to the engagement of mind and heart in our sung worship.

The majority of worshipers, especially our children, will sing from the poetry. Studies indicate that only about 27% of church goers read music anyway. Even those of us who do, when we use the hymnal in our private devotions, we will likely meditate from the column that looks like poetry where the progression of thought and rich poetic conventions are uninterrupted by the musical notation.

Let's restore the hymnal to Christian worship. Let's return to a format that is consistent with how Christians have sung in worship since the Reformation itself—poetry and meaning first, music second. This will send a clear message to the worshiper that the meaning of the words, taken on the lips, in the heart, and understood in the mind, is of first importance in our worship.

15

HIP OR HOLY

The Bonds have a family signal when someone is using an inappropriate tone of voice. "TOV check," my wife or I will say; check your tone of voice.

A curious function of language is that we can say the same words but with different inflections and they mean something entirely different. "Nice dress," can mean the beginning of a genuine compliment of my wife's new dress. Change the inflection, however, and the same words expressed in a sarcastic tone, mean the very opposite, an insult not a compliment.

In communication, the tone we set with our voices matters enormously to the meaning. I have felt like an unwelcome outsider peering in someone else's window in a service ostensibly of worship because there is a tone set by the pastor or music leader that acts almost like a secret hand shake, the initiates, the insiders, they're in on the mystery, but those of us who are visiting just don't get it.

Ours is a world of commercial branding, where businesses, institutions, and even churches will spend great quantities of time and money establishing their brand. And the tone set in a church's service will reflect the self-conceived branding identity of that church.

Make no mistake about it. Celebrity and entertainment drive this ship.

Let's be honest, we all want to be accepted. We want to be unique, ourselves, whom we perceive ourselves to be, and we desperately want to be esteemed by others, the more likes and friend requests the better.

Put another way, we all want to be cool. We want others to think we're pretty special, that we do things with style, the right kind of style, cool style, hip style. "Not your grandmother's church," some churches proudly describe themselves, seemingly oblivious to the afront such a marketing slogan is to the elderly, whom we are called to honor. It's part of their branding. It sets them apart from the other churches, you know, the embarrassing ones, the uncool, the unhip ones.

One could make the argument that this is true of all churches. But there is a particularly self-conscious doing of it in the hipster-cool church. When Mars Hill was a thing in nearby Seattle a few years back, and a number of my graduates were attending—my two eldest children studying at universities in Seattle were also attending— as a responsible Christian, I had to investigate.

I will never forget standing in the lobby of a strip-club-turned-church holding my toddler in my arms; Gillian may have been drooling on my shoulder. Halting in his tracks several yards away, the campus pastor stared at me, his mouth agape, just stared, as if he could not believe his eyes. Here was a man then in his late forties, gray hair, white shirt, coat and tie. Mars Hill was a church carefully branded to attract nineteen to twenty-nine-year-olds. What was a man like me doing there? I did not fit the demographic, and this campus pastor couldn't get it to compute. I finally walked over to him, extended my hand, and introduced myself. I felt like an outsider, to put it mildly. I didn't know the handshake. I didn't fit the brand.

PRIDE AND POWER

Yet, the all-excusing rationale behind this hip branding is evangelism. Some intercity cool churches have and are reaching a demographic of the lost, a connection to which some of the rest of us simply do not have. I know dear people who became Christians under the ministry of and were married by Mark Driscoll, all under the hipster ethos of the Mars Hill brand. But none of them are still there. Mars Hill is not still there. It is defunct. It collapsed under the insupportable weight of its own branding.

Why? Because hipster branding requires a celebrity. You must have a cool pastor for it work. But cultural relevance is an ever-moving target. Trends and fads change. And hipster pastors get gray hair—or lose it altogether. Not cool. What's more, once-cool dudes, as they age, look even more ridiculous preaching in jeans and a hoodie. The brand tarnishes over time. It's inevitable.

Still more pernicious, celebrity pastors are easily tempted to swagger, to be trend setters, to be with-it, like in the music industry. Spurgeon observed that

"When a man admires himself, he never adores God." We can't have it both ways. Over time, however much we keep insisting it's all about the gospel, self-admiration rears its head and devours the message.

Hard on the heels of this pride, is power. And pride and power kill churches and scatter the flock.

There are other versions of branding. One friend of mine in frustration described his church as "intellectual-seeker-friendly." This may be worse than hipster-cool-friendly, but both have played into the Devil's strategy: pride of cool or pride of acumen, they both lead to a desire for more power. Hence, Mars Hill does not exist anymore. Pride and a tight-fisted grip on power led to its "steepling plunge."

GOD, YOU'RE SO COOL

Some in the culturally relevant spiritual world actually think that they are being like God, singing like God, when they are being cool. They want unbelievers to join them because it's just, like, so cool to be a Christian.

Lest any of my readers think I have only chosen the worst examples of contemporary singing, I'll share another, one that we can only hope lies in the putrid bottom of the barrel. Ironically, it's from the land that gave us centuries of our rich English hymnody. Disclaimer: This is a real song. I did not make it up as a spoof.

God, You're so cool
There's no-one else
No, there's no-one else like you
God, you're so cool

And that is why I love you so much

This Vineyard UK Kids Worship song goes on repeating "God, you're so cool" twenty-nine times, if I didn't lose count. It says very little else.

Entertainment and hipster cool, that birthed such a frivolous ditty, may prove over time to be a marriage made in the abyss. Putting on the hipster tone, is like an oncologist who says to his patient, "I'm going to contract cancer so I can cure you of cancer." To put on cool, one must also put on pride, a public performance that requires a posture and tone that seem strangely inimical to the gospel. This insider cool branding disenfranchises the uninitiated, or unwittingly exerts pressure to conform. Then comes the disconcerting realization that someone who is not with-it is attempting to act like they are.

Hipster preaching, worship leading, music making creates an atmosphere that says Christianity, our version, our brand, is really fashionable. However much it is insisted that "It's all about Jesus," the tone of voice, as it were, employed by the ethos of the hipster church, and future iterations thereof, places its brand at the center, or its celebrity pastor, or cool band—thereby usurping the central place reserved for King Jesus alone.

PERPETUAL IMMATURITY

While speaking at a conference in Washington DC, I had the privilege of meeting Baltimore inner city pastor Carleton McLeod. After reading all the church-growth books he could get his hands on, he planted a church in the neediest part of Baltimore. Several years into that church's growth, he had a sudden realization.

Pastor McLeod described how cool a dude he used be, or tried to be; he preached in jeans, his shirt untucked, ball cap reversed, and, center-stage, was the hip-hop band. But after several years, studying his flock, it struck him; he had been "attempting to pull young people out of the kingdom of darkness with all the world's methods." God had been gracious and young people had been brought to a living faith in Christ. "But they'd stayed like children. By entertaining them, I had ensured they would remain immature."

Motivated by the Word, this pastor changed his ethos. Abandoning the entertaining performance that had been the central feature of worship, he began "...speaking the truth in love," to his congregation. Why? Because "...we are to grow up in all aspects into him who is the head, even Christ (Ephesians 4:15). Growing up means leaving some things behind. And the grown up looks back and realizes how good it was to leave them there. Immature people keep longing for the days of their youth, to be kids again, to find some new way of being cool.

There are times when unbelievers recognize the problem better than we Christians. Journalist David Brooks, in an article in the New York Times, wrote, "In reality, the people who live best tie themselves down. They don't ask: What cool thing can I do next? They ask: What is my responsibility here?"

Yet, the entertainment ethos persists in asking, what cool thing can we do next? Wearing ourselves out, scrambling after the latest thing precludes us from appreciating and learning from the wisdom and experience of the past. Kids fixate on the here-and-now. Mature adults value the enduring things.

J. I. Packer posed the question: "Why do we need the Puritans? The answer, in one word," he said, "is maturity… The Puritans exemplified maturity; we don't." Perhaps another way to put it is Paul's way, "…when I became a man, I did away with childish things" (I Corinthians 13:11b).

Whatever we disagree on, there's no disputing that the tone and jargon of the hipster church is driven by youth culture, and clothing is a significant part of youthful branding.

In the Reformation, preachers covered themselves, hid their individual clothing tastes under a Geneva gown. Though gowns may do the opposite in today's world, mature Christian leaders never dress to draw attention to themselves and their individuality.

DRESS THE PART

But cool pastors wear the uniform; they clothe themselves for casual, youthful, or edgy non-conformity. Instead of helping the congregation gaze on the loveliness of Jesus Christ, it would appear that hipster pastors dress according to the dictates of what is cool. Rather than being discreet and avoiding drawing attention to themselves by what they wear, these men seem to dress for self-expression, some with piercings and prominent tattoos on display— adding a tie when it feels good to do so. Why not?

In this context, wearing a tie now and then is simply another way of being you: I felt like dressing up today. It was my decision, my self-expression, what felt cool to me this morning. Don't worry, next week it's football jersey, jeans, and Chuck Taylors—or black leather. As if to say, If I had an audience with King Jesus, I'd just wear whatever old thing I felt like wearing.

One ABC reporter doing a story on a large celebrity church in New York City appraised the audience's response to the fashion-forward outfit and the cool carriage of the pastor, and concluded he was more of "a hipster heartthrob" than a pastor.

Deeply desiring to speak the truth in love, I am, nevertheless, compelled to say that this brand of Christianity and its derivations, however well intentioned, is trendy, youth-culture, celebrity-driven, and immature. Hailing from Grunge-capital Seattle, just across the Puget Sound from my home, celebrity pastor Mark Driscoll epitomized and popularized this breezy, cool, pulpiteering manner, all in the name of being all things to all people, so long as they were nineteen to twenty-nine, or tried to act like they were. And thousands of young, restless pastors and churches, some with passionate gospel motives, who have known no other ethos, persist in trying to clothe Christianity in the garb of cool.

COOL OR CHRISTIAN

Co-opting the entertainment ethos as many churches have done, has brought some large hipster churches to the attention of the mainstream media. And they're not all critical.

"The music! The lights! The crowds!" gushed a reporter on a CNN segment after a visit to 8,000-member Hillsong NYC. "It looks like a rock concert. And the lines around the block are enough to make any nightclub envious."

Sophisticated, men's high-end fashion and lifestyle magazine *GQ* imbedded a reporter, Taffy Brodesser-Akner, in a Hillsong worship service "to find out if Christianity can really be this cool and still be Christian." Studying the 8,000 attendees entering the worship center, including Justin Bieber, Akner gave her first impression: "It's where the cool kids spend Sunday morning after Saturday night at the club." The *GQ* journalist continued, "the singing is hot-breathed and sexy-close into microphones." But she wrote, "It made my body feel confused." After listening to the singing for a while (there's more music on the stage than anything else going on in most cool churches), Akner's assessment was that the songs had "melodies that all resemble one another, pleasingly, like spa music." She admitted to being drawn into the ethos, at least to some extent, by songs that "call to mind deeply sincere love songs."

Though not falling on her knees in repentance, by any stretch, Akner's over-all assessment was tentatively positive. She even confessed to wanting to raise her hands the morning after her visit to Hillsong. But not everybody who comes agrees, and not everybody stays.

"Hillsong has done for Christian music," wrote feminist writer Tanya Levin, former Hillsong Church member now atheist, "what the Dixie Chicks did for country and western: made it blond, sexy, and mainstream."

Put another way, they made it seem cool.

CLEVER DEVIL

Does anyone actually think that if God came down, he would dress that way, talk that way, sing that way? Would God sing "hot-breathed and sexy-close into microphones"? Would God our Maker "who gives songs in the night" (Job 35:20) sing those songs in anything that could remotely be labeled "sexy and mainstream"? None of this is God's way. It seems blasphemous even to consider it.

Would God inflect the way some cool pastors inflect? You've heard it, the perpetual up lilt, as if every statement is a question; it sounds so breezy and urbane, as if to say that you alone have come to pose the questions no one else is asking. What's more, by your seeming spontaneity that showcases your cleverness and wit, you let others know that the answers come easily for you.

God, for whom alone answers do come easily, doesn't talk that way. His voice does not sound that way, he does not sing that way. It's as if we think he ought to, but there is zero biblical evidence that God, who is "a consuming fire," takes a casual, cool, hipster approach to anything. Nor should we.

"Preacher, give up trying to be cool," wrote Southern Seminary President Al Mohler. "Cool changes so quickly... Do what cool can't do. Bathe your heart and mind in the ancient Scriptures. Devote yourself to proclaiming the eternal truth of God."

A heart bathed in God's holy Word produces one thing. A heart bathed in pop entertainment and celebrity culture produces quite another. One cannot have it both ways.

Even agnostics Strunk and White, in their classic book on writing, understood that an affected and artificial tone of voice and manner of communicating was indicative of pride: "Do not affect a breezy manner. The breezy style is often the work of the egocentric." They strongly suggest avoiding "uninhibited prose" that "creates high spirits."

The "breezy manner" sounds suspiciously like the hipster cool voice in the pulpit on the stage. These egocentric pretentions place the author, the pastor, or the music leader at the center. This comes so naturally to the entertainment ethos because that's how it all works. The performer on the stage is there to perform, and the fawning crowd are there to be amused, to take for themselves, to be entertained. It's how it works, regardless of the words. Remember, most of us don't listen to the words.

The focus of breezy entertainment is me-centered. The focus of worship is God-centered, and there is no place for breezy when entering the presence of the living and holy God.

There were versions of entertainment evangelism long before anyone used the term hipster (a term that may outlive its cool status soon enough). Even in Charles Spurgeon's day. "The Devil has seldom done a cleverer thing," he wrote, "than hinting to the Church that part of their mission is to provide entertainment for the people, with a view to winning them."

A DANGEROUS PLACE

However in step with the popular culture entertainment worship may be, it is profoundly out of step with the Bible. Like his Father, Jesus was not cool. The Son of God was so radically out of step with the culture around him that viscous critics tore off his robes, flogged him until his naked back was raw and bloody, and then they nailed him to a cross, suspended him in mockery and shame, and crucified him, the world looking on, deriding and making sport of him. No, Jesus was not cool. The world hated him.

Holding the hipster approach to worship and singing up next to the persecuted church further unmasks the fallacy of cool. It is not cool to be a Christian in Nigeria today, or China—the list is long. Imagine the bewilderment of any of our brethren in the persecuted church as they try to get their minds around the notion that it's cool to be a Christian, at least cool if you identify with our brand. They would likely think that it was something else altogether, not the Christianity they experience. It would seem ten million miles from the cost of following Christ in their bloody world.

"Consumer-based, me-centered, music-driven, reductionistic, therapeutic, and theologically vacuous Christianity," wrote Gospel Reformation Network Executive Coordinator Jon D. Payne, "is ten million miles from the real thing. It mirrors the world more than Scripture."

There's little argument that no single entity has more shaped music-driven, entertainment worship in recent decades than Australian mega-church Hillsong. In a period of just eighteen months, there were 760,000,000 downloads of Hillsong songs, creating vast sums of money for the writers of those songs. Amidst a wave of apostacy among high-profile church leaders, one of Hillsong's songwriters, Marty Sampson, joined in the trend. "I'm genuinely losing my faith … and it doesn't bother me."

It ought to bother the Church, however, when a key contributor to the lyrical content of what millions of professing Christians sing in worship says of the gospel, "it's not for me. I am not in anymore."

Dr. Payne helps us connect the dots. "It's no wonder, then, why so many celebrity pastors and leaders are abandoning the faith for the idols and approval of our culture. It's the culture, not objective truth, that has been chiefly shaping their thinking all along." Pew Research Center findings concur, but it's not just celebrity leaders abandoning the faith. In our rapidly secularizing society, there's a spiraling decline of people willing to identify themselves as Christians.

Some might hasten to dismiss Payne's conclusions; after all, he's a conservative, confessional Presbyterian. He's got a liturgical agenda. Perhaps more will listen when someone deeply invested in the entertainment industry is forced to come to the same conclusions.

Lead vocalist and bassist for the Grammy-nominated band Skillet, John L. Cooper put it this way: "We must stop making worship leaders… or cool people, or 'relevant' people the most influential people in

Christendom." He readily applies this to himself. "[W]e are in a dangerous place when the Church is looking to twenty-year-old worship singers as our source of truth. We now have a church culture that learns who God is from singing modern praise songs rather than from the teachings of the Word."

Cooper describes why musicians can gain so much power over the Church. "If you look the right way, if you sing the right way, if you sound the right way, you can become an extremely powerful person in today's culture, because, unfortunately, the Church is looking to be entertained." He candidly admits the limitations of many in the music industry.

> ...singers and musicians are good at communicating emotion and feeling... However, singers are not always the best people to write solid Bible truth and doctrine. Sometimes we are too young, too ignorant of Scripture, too unaware, or too unconcerned about the purity of Scripture and the holiness of the God we are singing to.

All this from a consummate entertainer, but who has come to realize the vast limitations of what he does. We now have an entire generation of people who only have experienced the entertainment ethos of which Cooper has become so self-critical. What is the result to this and the next generation of those who call themselves Christians? We know how to behave at a rock concert or a football game. Ignorant of what is appropriate, however, we no longer know how to behave in the household of God.

HOW TO BEHAVE

In the 1st century, new Christians knew how to behave at the theater, or a chariot race at the circus. Surrounded by his entertainment-driven world, the Apostle Paul wanted the Church to be discerning. He was in earnest that they "…know how one ought to behave in the household of God, which is the Church of the living God, a pillar and buttress of the truth" (I Timothy 3:15).

How are we to behave in the household of God? In the Church of the living God? A pillar and buttress of the truth? Nowhere does Paul say, go imitate the Greco-Roman world's entertainment. Why not? Because it is inappropriate to the household of God. It is not God's way. It is not God's tone of voice, heard and known on every page of Holy Scripture.

What did God say to Lot when he cast his eyes toward the plain and sojourned in Sodom? What did he say to the Israelites about Egypt? What does he say to us about being holy, being set apart? "Come out of her, my people, lest you take part in her sins" (Revelation 18:4).

Before the Reformation, 16th century Geneva was a city-state amusing itself to death. In entertainment-crazed Geneva, John Calvin faced pressures from those who wanted a Renaissance version of entertainment to shape Christian worship. His response is apropos for the temptation in every age to conform to a worldly ethos and still call it worship. "God does not intend there to be churches as places for people to make merry and laugh in, as if a comedy

234

were being acted here. There must be majesty in his Word, by which we may be moved and affected."

Worship that apes entertainment priorities can give us a feeling of being moved and affected, but if our affections are not first humbled before the majesty of the Word of God, it's all a cheat. Our devotion to entertainment in our worship may prove to be a monument to our distrust of the power of the Word. We want something else, something new and exciting, to move and affect us. We want the world not the Word.

God alone moves hearts by the means which he alone has ordained. When we supplant his means with our methods, make no mistake, we're still worshiping, but the object of our adoration may be the work of our own hands, the god of entertainment not the God of the Word.

FAKE NEWS

At the end of the day, we must reject the entertainment ethos, not because it is so powerful. But because it is so weak. Pop music can do so little. It leaves us with a mono voice. We can be emotive, our affections stimulated. It is capable of giving us a spiritual-seeming high, putting us in the zone. But all this may be artificial, fake news, not gospel good news. Pop music can make us feel good, but it falls far short of making us feel bad.

Just as some rock and roll was limited to three chords, so the array of pop genre is vastly limited. It can't do deep and searching lamentation. It is incapable of renewing the mind, ennobling the heart, and awakening the deeper affections. We may find that we have been asking the equivalent of a comic book to do what only

Shakespeare can do; "God, you're so cool" to do what only "Praise, my soul, the King of heaven" can do.

Pop entertainment music does immediate gratification very well; but, by idolizing the passions, it is incapable of lifting us above ourselves to the grandeur of God's holiness. We've emptied our resources. With pop music, we've shot our wad. We have nothing else in our kit. No majesty, no grandeur, just therapeutic cool, over and over again.

Impoverished by the loss of grandeur, we don't know how to sing in church, we don't know how to sing at a deathbed, a funeral, even a wedding. By what Lewis called "chronological snobbery," thinking we've finally arrived, we now have all the answers; we have cut ourselves off from the great canon of music and lyric that the household of God has been singing for nearly two millennia, cut off by cool and the entertainment ethos.

CONTENT NOT COOL

Sometimes the way forward, is to halt, stop in our tracks, turn about-face. It's called repentance: Stop what you're doing, turn around and behave "how one ought to behave in the household of God, which is the Church of the living God, a pillar and buttress of the truth" (I Timothy 3:15). Repentance begins when we stop caring about being cool.

Lamenting at the Church and her bondage to entertainment worship, scholar L. Joseph Herbert, Jr. posed the question: "In a world ringing with noise and suffused with artful idolizing of passions divorced from objective [truths], where are we to find melodies capable of penetrating our hardened hearts with spiritual truths?"

Where, indeed? We think repentance means giving up good things, that God wants us joyless. But the marvelous thing about true repentance is that it frees us from bondage to counterfeit joy. We no longer have to be enslaved to the latest thing, to what is deemed relevant—at the moment. We are free from pride, self-aggrandizement, and the pursuit of power. We are free to begin discovering those melodies and hymns that are capable of penetrating our hearts, renewing our minds, and lifting us above the banal, the transient, the vacuous. Now, freed from the tyranny of cool, we can be content.

Welsh poet, Anna L. Waring, was little known in a lifetime that spanned much of the 19th century. What she was known for was not wanting to be known. Quietly and humbly, she spent her days going into the filthy prison in Bristol, a hell hole like the ones Charles Dickens exposed in his novels. In the despair and darkness of those cells, Waring shone the light of the gospel of Jesus Christ to the condemned, some as young as ten years old. And she wrote poetry, hymn lyrics you will rarely if ever hear sung in the cool church.

I ask thee for the daily strength,
To none who ask denied,
A mind to blend with outward life,
While keeping at thy side...

Waring's is a poetic voice crying in our liturgical wilderness. Concluding the stanza, she encapsulates the way forward, the escape from cool:

Content to fill a little space,
If thou be glorified.

Once we return to contentment with the richness of the ordinary means of grace (so stupendously extraordinary)—prayer, praise, Word, and sacrament—the gracious means by which God alone is glorified in our worship, we can unmask the artificial splendor of the glitz and glamor of the entertainment ethos, then we are free to rise and worship. Content now, all the commercially driven delights that demand our devotion and our dollars behind us, we are free and can lift our voices with the ancient Irish hymn writer, "Riches I heed not, nor man's empty praise... Thou and thou only, first in my heart..."

We can't have it both ways. The world's glitter and entertainment require the first place in our hearts. Everything demands it. Entertainment is preeminent. Yet it is the unchallenged assumption of an entire generation of Christians that we cannot do worship without its ethos. I fear it might prove to be the reverse.

The Apostle Paul knew that we cannot worship unless Christ is in the first place, unless Christ is preeminent in all things (Colossians 1:18b). Entertainment feels the same way. Which will it be for us, Christ's preeminence or entertainment's? We must make our choice, the tempting voice of entertainment, the empty glory of the world's methods, or Christ himself? I think 16th century German Lutheran pastor Johann Franck made the right choice, and so must we:

Hence with earthly treasure!
Thou art all my pleasure,
Jesus, all my choice.
Hence, thou empty glory!
Naught to me thy story,
Told with tempting voice.
Pain or loss or shame or cross
Shall not from my Savior move me,
Since he deigns to love me.

APPENDIX

New Reformation Hymns

I am thrilled that God has raised up in recent years gifted hymn writers and composers to help lead us into greener liturgical pastures. When future Church historians are laboring to chronicle this moment in redemptive history, I am confident that names like James Montgomery Boyce, R. C. Sproul, Stuart Townend, the Gettys, and others will be seen as having contributed to a critical mass, the catalysts needed to turn sung worship back to Christ-exalting, God-honoring, psalm-like, substantive praise. Rather than sit back and play the critic, with fear and trepidation, I felt myself compelled to set pen to paper and make what contribution I am able to the joyful task. Hence, the following, New Reformation Hymns. SDG

Come Bless the Lord

"I saw the Lord sitting upon a throne, high and lifted up; and the
train of his robe filled the temple."
Isaiah 6:1

Come, bless the Lord and trembling rise
Before the Sovereign of the skies;
Before his majesty now raise
Adoring hymns of grateful praise!

Bow humbly down, your sins confess;
Pour out your soul, on mercy rest.
Since Christ triumphant bears your woe,
Repent, his cleansing mercy know.

Rise joyful now and Jesus bless
For his imputed righteousness,
His sovereign kindness, lavished grace,
His freely dying in your place.

Pay all your vows and cheerful bring
The gifts he gave; give back to him.
His gifts, so vast, his life outpoured—
Ourselves we lay before you, Lord.

Come, Word of Life, yourself reveal;
Your truth make us to know and feel;
Inflame our minds to love your ways;
Make us a sacrifice of praise.

Come, Jesus Christ, sweet heav'nly Bread,
And with your life this table spread,
Then grateful we will solemn dine
On hallowed bread and sacred wine.

Now go into the world in peace,
And bear the burdens of the least,
And bathe your neighbors' feet in love,
So Christ they'll know and praise above.

Douglas Bond, © June 4, 2008

Creator God, Our Sovereign Lord

"I am the way, and the truth, and the life. No one comes to the
Father except through me." John 14:6 *Sola Scriptura, sola gratia, sola fide,
solus Christus, soli Deo gloria.*

Creator God, our Sovereign Lord,
The heavens tell, the stars have shown,
Your splendor, might, and Deity,
But Truth lies in your Word alone.
    My heart to you, O God, I give,
    And by your Word I live.

In Truth your Word reveals my guilt,
My lost, unworthy self makes known,
But now made new I'm justified
And live and move by Faith alone.
    My heart to you, O God, I give,
    And now by Faith I live.

Before you made the world you chose,
In love, to send your only Son
To ransom me and make me one
With Christ, my Lord, by Grace alone.
    My heart to you, O God, I give,
    And now by Grace I live.

O Christ, Redeemer, Savior, King,
Subdued by grace, I am your own;
Enthrall my soul and make me free,
Reformed, redeemed by Christ alone.
    My heart to you, O God, I give,
    And now in Christ I live.

O glorious God, who reigns on high,
With heart in hand, before your throne,
We hymn your glory 'round the world
With psalms adoring you alone.
    My heart to you, O God, I give
    And for your glory live.

Douglas Bond, © October 31, 2007

His Name Above the Highest Name

"Therefore God has highly exalted him and bestowed on him the name that is above every name, so that at the name of Jesus every knee should bow, in heaven and on earth and under the earth, and every tongue confess that Jesus Christ is Lord, to the glory of God the Father." Philippians 2:9-11

His Name above the highest Name:
With hymns we hail the loud refrain,
Majestic Name of God proclaim,
Of Jesus, Lord, for sinners slain!

The Lord, Most High, the great I Am,
The Father has the Son ordained
To ransom children he has named
As heir of his eternal reign.

The Lamb of God, his worthy Name,
In him our restless souls find rest,
His chosen loved ones he reclaimed,
From all eternity the blessed.

The Shepherd seeks his flock to save,
To rescue us from sin and shame,
Stoops down and lifts me from the grave,
And calls me by his powerful Name.

My name's inscribed upon his hands,
His nail-pierced hands atonement made;
My Lord's fulfilled his Laws demands,
And with his Life my debt has paid.

One day, the doomed will bow the knee,
Their rebel tongues confess with shame,
As gnashing to the mountains flee
The terrible glory of the Name.

O, how majestic is your Name!
We shout your worth—in all the earth—
With joyful hymns—our hearts aflame—
With glorious splendor of the Name!

Douglas Bond, © 2019

How Blessed the One Who Fears the Lord

"The fear of the Lord is the beginning of wisdom, and
the knowledge of the Holy One is understanding."
Proverbs 9:10

How blessed the man who fears the Lord!
Who daily feeds upon his Word,
And falls down at the mercy seat,
And casts his fears at Jesus' feet.

How blessed is she who fears the Lord!
Delighting, trusting in his Word:
She fears no danger, threat, or harm
While resting safe in Jesus' arms.

How blessed are sons who fear the Lord!
Who hear and heed the Spirit's Word.
No tyrant's heel can hurt them here
Since they the Sovereign Lord revere.

How blessed when daughters fear the Lord!
And love God's ways, his holy Word.
Disease and dying hold no fear
Since Christ who conquered death is near.

How blessed the home that fears the Lord!
Adoring the incarnate Word;
Like cherubim and seraphim,
In humble awe, God's praises hymn.

How blessed the church that fears the Lord!
Her Savior's work, her sure reward;
With wondrous voice, high praise repeats,
And bows in awe at Jesus' feet.

Douglas Bond, © December 28, 2017

I Know That My Redeemer Lives

"For I know that my Redeemer lives, and at the last
he will stand upon the earth." Job 19:25

I know that my Redeemer lives!
And with his life my sin forgives.
O Jesus, Lord, I'll hope and pray,
And patient be—though come what may.

When troubles come with grief and tears
And hope is lost in all my fears,
On God who gives and takes away
My sins, and doubts, and sorrows lay.

His ways are wondrous, high above,
So full of righteousness and love.
So glorious is my God of grace,
My longing heart leaps from its place.

Redeeming mercy gives me light
And songs of joy within the night.
Since Jesus all my troubles bore,
I am God's friend forevermore!

O great Redeemer, glorious sight!
Your will and ways are always right.
My heart within me yearns to see
Your glory, light, and majesty!

Douglas Bond, © December, 2010

If I Can Speak With Tongues of Fire

"If I speak in the tongues of men and of angels, but
have not love, I am a noisy gong or a clanging cymbal."
I Corinthians 13:1

If I can speak in tongues of fire
Yet fail to do what love requires,
I'm nothing—though high mountains move—
I'm nothing without perfect love.

I'm nothing if I try to hide
Resentment, envy, selfish pride.
I'm nothing—though high myst'ries find—
If I'm not patient, humble, kind.

His heav'nly gifts God gives to me
So Christ's perfected love I'd see
And know—and speak, and serve and give—
And in my holy Bridegroom live.

In faith and hope, love perseveres,
No anger and no rudeness hears;
Such lovingkindness—fully blessed—
Gives foretastes of eternal rest.

I see in part like children here,
A poor reflection in a mirror;
Yet in my heart I long to find
Love more by Jesus' love refined.

Above I'll know, as Christ has known,
How vast his love for sinners shown!
With eyes undimmed I'll end my race
And gaze on Jesus face to face!
Douglas Bond, © December 28, 2007

Jesus, Faithful Friend of Sinners

"The Son of Man came eating and drinking, and they say, 'Here is a glutton and a drunkard, a friend of tax collectors and sinners.'" Matthew 11:19a

Jesus, faithful Friend of sinners,
God incarnate, pure and sinless;
I am full of all that hinders,
Empty, lonely, lost and friendless.

Jesus, tender Shepherd faithful,
God in fullness here below;
I am anxious, dull, ungrateful,
Prone to wander, full of woe.

Jesus, Servant, precious treasure,
Gave your life my life to win.
I am vain, pursuing pleasure,
Full of hunger, self and sin.

Jesus, Savior, blessed Redeemer-
Filled with mercy overflowing,
I'm forgiven without measure,
Friend of sinners, glorious King!

Douglas Bond, © October 25, 2014

King Jesus Reigns

"Therefore render to Caesar the things that are
Caesar's, and to God the things that are God's."
Matthew 22:21

King Jesus reigns, enthroned on high!
With heart and voice we glorify
His Majesty, his power and grace,
And his high sovereignty embrace.

Though kings usurp and proud men try
Their pompous selves to deify,
Adoring praise shall never cease
For Christ, Redeemer, Prince of Peace!

King Jesus rules upon his throne
And does the wealth of nations own;
While fading things to Caesar bring,
Ourselves we render to our King.

While pharaohs, kings, and emperors boast,
The King of kings leads out his host;
The proud, one day, shall bow the knee
When Christ in triumph sets us free!

King Jesus wears his worthy crown,
Though envious men and nations frown,
And we, by grace, on eagle's wings,
Uphold the Crown rights of our King!

His holy nation, chosen ones,
We joyful bow, and with our tongues
We hymn allegiance high and sing,
"Hail Jesus! Sovereign Lord and King!"

Douglas Bond, © March 12, 2008

Lord Jesus, You're More Excellent

"Christ has obtained a ministry that is as much more excellent
than the old as the covenant he mediates is better." Hebrews 8:6

Lord Jesus, you're more excellent
Than Moses' ancient covenant:
God's Law you perfectly obeyed
And on the cross its curse you paid.

My Royal Priest is excellent
Above the dying priests who went
In yearly terror through the veil—
But once for all Christ did prevail.

Lord Jesus, you're more excellent
Than all the guardian angels sent
To guide our steps both day and night,
Since Jesus guards with sovereign might.

Great Savior, you're more excellent
Than all the Devil's arrows spent
In furious rage against the ones
For whom Christ died to make his sons.

Kind Jesus, you're more excellent
Than doubts and troubles I invent;
Your life laid down, my victory won—
My Advocate, God's holy Son.

O Christ, you are most excellent,
By th'new and better covenant:
Redeeming Love who took my part,
Inscribed your Law upon my heart.

O Righteous One, most excellent,
Your cross fulfilled the covenant;
O Worthy One, who took my place,
I long to see you face to face.

Douglas Bond, © March 28, 2011

¡Oh Cristo! Tú Eres Superior

¡Oh Cristo! Tú eres superior
Al pacto de Moisés, Señor:
Cumplió la Ley Tu perfección,
Tu cruz pagó su maldición.

Mi Sacerdote es superior
Al que anualmente, con terror
El velo había de cruzar;
De una vez Cristo iba a triunfar.

¡Oh Cristo! Tú eres superior
Al ángel que es mi protector
De día y al anochecer;
Jesús nos guarda con poder.

Salvador, Tú eres superior
Al dardo del engañador
Lanzado en ira contra aquel
Al que el Señor mantiene fiel.

Mi Cristo, Tú eres superior
A mis problemas y a mi error;
Tu entrega me hizo vencedor;
Tú, mi abogado y defensor.

¡Oh Cristo! Tú eres superior,
Tu pacto es nuevo y es mejor:
Manifestó amor redentor,
Grabó Tu Ley en mi interior.

¡Oh el Justo! Tú eres superior,
De un mejor pacto eres fiador;
¡Oh el Digno! Muerto en mi lugar,
Tu rostro anhelo contemplar.

Douglas Bond, © 2019
Spanish translation, David Rivero
Versified, Santiago Miguez

My Soul Exults In God the Lord

"I will greatly rejoice in the Lord; my soul shall exult in
my God, for he has clothed me with the garments of
salvation; he has covered me with the robe of
righteousness..." Isaiah 61:10

My soul exults in God the Lord,
The Light arising, radiant Word!
The wealth of nations Yahweh brings
And clothes his children like we're kings.

My heart exults in God the Lord,
Redeemer, Savior, glorious Word!
He binds the broken-hearted's sores
And bursts the captive's prison doors.

My soul exults in Christ the Lord,
Eternal God, majestic Word!
The oil of gladness on their head,
The mourning poor are richly fed.

My heart exults in God the Lord,
Subduing King, the faithful Word!
The least becomes a mighty clan,
The branch and planting of God's hand.

My soul exults in Christ the Lord,
Our Bridegroom Jesus, Righteous Word!
You clothe your bride in beauty's dress,
The robes of your own righteousness.

My heart is thrilled with God the Lord,
My Comfort, King, and Conquering Word!
Your open gates rich love displays,
Salvation's walls resound with praise!

Douglas Bond, © August 27, 2016

O Love of God, Exalted High

"…so that Christ may dwell in your hearts through faith—that you, being rooted and grounded in love, may have strength to comprehend with all the saints what is the breadth and length and height and depth, and to know the love of Christ that surpasses knowledge, that you may be filled with all the fullness of God." Ephesians 3:17-19

O love of God, exalted high,
Transcends the earth, the sea, the sky.
O Father now I bow my knee
Before your loving majesty.
All praise we render to the Son,
The Father, Spirit, Three-in-One.

According to your lavished grace,
Sweet Heav'nly Dove, my heart embrace;
Renewing life within my soul,
With fullness filled and love controlled.
All praise to Jesus, Holy Son,
The Father, Spirit, Three-in-One.

O love of Christ, surpassing wide,
For wayward sinners prone to hide;
Love's reach extends to every land,
To every country, every clan.
All praise we render, gracious Son,
The Father, Spirit, Three-in-One.

Elect from love-forsaken tribes,
Their names upon his hand inscribed,
Will with triumphant hosts above
Extol his wide-embracing love!
All praise we render to the Son,
The Father, Spirit, Three-in-One.

The love of Jesus, broad and deep:

Through death's dark valleys still he keeps
And guards my heart against the foe,
Through depths of sorrow, loss, and woe.
All praise to Christ, eternal Son,
The Father, Spirit, Three-in-One.

O love of God, how vast and long!
No demon might or tyrant throng
Can snatch me from my Father's hand
Or thwart his love-bought sovereign plan.
All praise to Christ, exalted Son,
The Father, Spirit, Three-in-One.

Douglas Bond, © March 7, 2015

Our God, In All Things Works for Good

"And we know that for those who love God all
things work together for good, for those who are called
according to his purpose." Romans 8:28

Our God in all things works for good;
His sovereign, gracious will has stood
And will through endless ages stand,
Sustained and ordered by his hand.

In goodness God stretched out the sky,
The sun and moon and stars that cry,
"Almighty God has made all things!"—
Creation groans yet shouts and sings.

From heaven's bounty God gives food
To saint and rebel, bad and good;
Our God in all things meets men's needs
And just and unjust kindly feeds.

When clouds descend and troubles rise,
Despair and darkness, tears and sighs,
Yet God is good in grief and loss,
And bears his own who bear their cross.

Redemption, purchased and applied
To favored ones for whom Christ died;
His lambs he grants repentance free
And eyes of faith his cross to see.

All praise to God who works for good!
Whose loving kindness firm has stood
And will through endless ages stand,
Unerring, ordered by his hand.
                Douglas Bond, © May 15, 2006

The Lord, Great Sovereign

"Then the Lord will appear over them, and his arrow will
go forth like lightning; the Lord God will sound the
trumpet..." Zechariah 9:14

The Lord, Great Sovereign, shall appear,
His wand'ring sheep he'll bring
From distant lands, through surging seas,
To shout before their King!

Deceitful shepherds, false and vain,
Have led his flock astray;
God's enemies he'll trample down,
Their lies he will repay.

With trumpet blast, the Lord appears,
His arrows flashing round;
He shields his flock, destroys his foes;
Glad vict'ry shouts will sound.

He makes his children mighty men,
They bend the battle bow;
So, in God's strength, against the proud,
His foes they overthrow!

Restored, victorious, gathered in,
Their enemies o'ercome;
God's children worship round his throne,
And in his name they run!

God's bless'd, redeemed, and chosen ones,
His children shout and sing!
"All praise to Christ, the Cornerstone,
Triumphant, glorious King!"

Douglas Bond, © 2001

The Lord Has Done Great Things for Them

"When the Lord restored the fortunes of Zion, we were like those who dream. Then our mouth was filled with laughter, and our tongue with shouts of joy; then they said among the nations, 'The Lord has done great things for them.' The Lord has done great things for us; we are glad." Psalm 126:1-3

"For he who is mighty has done great things for me, and holy is his name." Luke 1:49

'The Lord has done great things for them,'
In David's City Bethlehem;
The promised prophet, Zion's seed,
Restored our life as God decreed.

The scepter of the nations God's destroyed
And filled our tongues with shouts of joy!
The Lord has done great things for me,
Restored my faith and made me see!

'The Lord has done great things for them,'
Through Jesus' birth in Bethlehem;
Our great high priest of Jacob's seed,
Restored his heirs as God decreed.

The Prince of Peace, the holy seed,
Restored our hope by grace indeed.
The gladsome virgin bears God's Son!
'The Lord, for me, great deeds has done!'

'The Lord has done great things for them,'
Through Christ's low birth in Bethlehem;
The King of kings, the promised seed,
Restored his realm as God decreed.

You've brought us home with shouts of joy,
The serpent crushed, his sway destroyed;
The Lord has done great things for me!
Restored his love eternally!

Douglas Bond, © December 22, 2018

Triumphant Jesus

"Who shall bring any charge against God's elect? It
is God who justifies." Romans 8:33

Triumphant Jesus bore the cross
Of cruel passion, curse, and loss;
He routed sin, and death, and woe,
And Satan my infernal foe.

Yet does the fiend still prowl and lurk,
His schemes upon my heart to work.
But God before me who can stand
When Christ in battle guides my hand?

Since Christ my Savior works within,
No more am I a slave of sin.
The hopes of hell and Satan wrecked,
No more can he charge God's elect.

No power of flesh or demon's might
Can snatch from me Christ's blood-bought right.
I more than conquer by the Word
Of Christ my Captain and my Lord!

Douglas Bond, © December 12, 2007

We Marvel at Your Wondrous Word

"They will rebuild the ancient ruins and restore the places long
devastated; they will renew the ruined cities that have been
devastated for generations." Isaiah 61:4 *Sola Scriptura, sola gratia,
sola fide, solus Christus, soli Deo gloria*

We marvel at your wondrous Word,
Divinely breathed, the Spirit's sword.
Rebuild our ruins, restore our race,
O Living Word, the God of grace.

We need your Grace, the grace that brings
Forgiveness borne on mercy's wings.
Rebuild our ruins, restore our race,
O God of mercy, God of grace.

Believing Faith repentance brings
And joy that makes our glad hearts sing!
Rebuild our ruins, restore our race,
O faithful Jesus, God of grace.

We worship Christ and to him cling,
To him alone, for everything!
Rebuild our ruins, restore our race,
Messiah, Jesus, God of grace.

We Glory in the One who brings
Eternal peace—all glorious King!
Rebuild our ruins, restore our race,
O Sovereign Jesus, God of grace.

Douglas Bond, © January 2, 2015

We Rise and Worship

"Oh, taste and see that the Lord is good! Blessed is
the man who takes refuge in him!" Psalm 34:8

We rise and worship you, our Lord,
       With grateful hearts for grace outpoured,
For you are good—O taste and see—
       Great God of mercy rich and free.

A chosen son of God on high,
       I trembling bow and wonder why
This Sovereign Lord—O taste and see—
       In love stooped down and rescued me.

Your Son obeyed the Law for me,
       Then died my death upon the tree.
O Jesus Christ, I taste and see
       And marvel that you purchased me.

In might, your Spirit drew me in,
       My quickened heart from death to win.
O Holy Spirit—taste and see—
       My comfort, hope, and surety.

With thankful praise our hearts we give;
       By grace alone we serve and live.
O Trinity, we taste and see
       Your sovereign goodness full and free.

Douglas Bond, © November 19, 2007

We Worship Christ the Cornerstone

"...you are no longer strangers and aliens, but you are
fellow citizens with the saints and members of the
household of God, built on the foundation of the apostles
and prophets, Christ Jesus himself being the cornerstone..."
Ephesians 2:20-21

We worship Christ, the Cornerstone,
Who made us one in him alone!
Not Jew nor Gentile, bond nor free,
This commonwealth of unity.
Our Lord has from the two made one,
And with his blood our peace has won.

Brought near in Christ, the Prince of Peace,
Our envy, strife, and warfare cease;
For tribes and tongues, and strangers all,
Our Peace has broken down the wall;
New covenant mercy he extends
To us his fellow heirs and friends.

One faith, one hope of heav'n above,
A unity of holy love;
One body made of many parts,
A unity of loving hearts;
One temple built of cast-off stone,
Made holy by the Holy One.

To Jesus Christ we lift one voice—
The household of our Father's choice—
Whose love makes ours for others grow
And makes the watching world to know
That our abiding Cornerstone
Has made us one in Christ alone!

Douglas Bond, © December 2, 2009

What Wonder Filled the Starry Night

"…there were shepherds out in the field, keeping watch
over their flock by night. And an angel of the Lord appeared
to them, and the glory of the Lord shone around them, and
they were filled with great fear." Luke 2:8-9

What wonder filled the starry night
    When Jesus came with heralds bright!
I marvel at his lowly birth,
    That God for sinners stooped to earth.

His splendor laid aside for me,
    While angels hailed his Deity,
And shepherds on their knees in fright
    Fell down in wonder at the sight.

The child who is the Way, the Truth,
    Who pleased his Father in his youth,
Through all his days the Law obeyed,
    Yet for its curse his life he paid.

What drops of grief fell on the site
    Where Jesus wrestled through the night,
Then for transgressions not his own,
    He bore my cross and guilt alone.

What glorious Life arose that day
    When Jesus took death's sting away!
His children raised to life and light,
    To serve him by his grace and might.

One day the angel hosts will sing,
    "Triumphant Jesus, King of kings!"
Eternal praise we'll shout to him
    When Christ in splendor comes again!

Douglas Bond, © December 16, 2010

Hymn to Synergism

Anti-Hymn—What a hymn would sound like if
Jesus didn't pay it all and salvation was a responsible
partnership between God and sinners

I praise and worship Father thee
Since I have chosen free
To bow before your majesty
By my own liberty.
O God of fairness, with my voice,
I praise you for my choice!

The Father leaves us, every man,
To choose him if we can;
My will he never violates
But passive sits and waits.
O God of fairness, with my voice,
I praise you for my choice!

The Son who did his best for all
Leaves me alone to call;
Along with all the human race,
I'm left to choose my place.
O God of fairness, with my voice,
I praise you for my choice!

The Spirit draws—but not too much;
My will he'll never touch,
But leaves me free to choose my faith,
The captain of my fate.
O God of fairness, with my voice,
I praise you for my choice!

It would not make a bit of sense
To earn my recompense,
If I don't have ability,
My free will and my liberty.
O God of fairness, with my voice,
I praise you for my choice!

With apologies, Douglas Bond, © January 29, 2012

ACKNOWLEDGEMENTS

God Sings! is a collection of articles, lectures, sermons, and excerpts from some of my other books, all adapted and collected into a single volume, what I set out to say in my Mr. Pipes series but here in one book. I'm deeply indebted to many who have invested in me both theologically and literarily over the years. Above all, I am indebted to my mother and father, who instilled a love of books and reading in me, and supremely a love of The Book, the Word of God. Many of the hymns explored and analyzed herein I first sang in daily family worship as a boy sitting around the breakfast table. Additionally, I am indebted to my faithful advanced-review readers: James Hakim, John Schrupp, Tilly Hunter, and, best of all, my mother.

Douglas Bond, blessed husband, father of six, and grandfather of six and counting, is a hymn writer, an award-winning teacher, and author of twenty-eight books, several translated into Dutch, Portuguese, and Korean. He speaks internationally at churches, schools, and conferences, directs the Oxford Creative Writing Master Class, and leads Church history and hymn tours. Find out more at bondbooks.net.

Grace
Works!
(And Ways We Think It Doesn't)

"Diagnoses the tendency of even the most
biblical churches to drift into legalism."
—DR. JOEL R. BEEKE

DOUGLAS BOND

"Anyone familiar with Douglas Bond's other works will know him as a great storyteller. This book is about the greatest story of all: the gospel. Issuing from the faith of a recipient of God's good news and the care of a shepherd, any wounds inflicted here will be those of a friend. Grace is not the enemy of works but the only proper source. It's amazing how many ways we can get that wrong—usually, as Doug argues, by incremental and often imperceptible changes. There is a lot of wisdom in this book, but none greater than the wisdom that Christ is and gives us in his gospel."

MICHAEL HORTON, J. Gresham Machen Professor of Systematic Theology and Apologetics,

"*Grace Works* clearly shows how an emphasis on grace differentiates Christianity from all the works religions invented by man. Douglas Bond also explains well what happens when we decide the cake God gives us needs our own frosting: we get a sugar rush now and a stomach ache later."

MARVIN OLASKY, Editor-in-chief, WORLD News Group

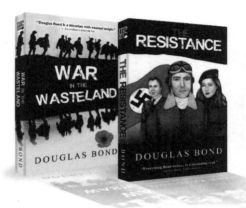

" *War in the Wasteland* is proof positive of what I have known for many years now: Douglas Bond is a great storyteller. Indeed, this novel combines all the attributes of a can't-put-it-down thriller with the intellectual tensions of a historical drama: taut plotting, strong characters, and soaring backdrop. Put this one on the top of your must-read list."

GEORGE GRANT, author, teacher, pastor at Parish Presbyterian Church

"If you enjoy inspirational war stories, flying, intrigue, mystery, and intense anticipation, you will love Douglas Bond's new book *The Resistance*. Not only is the action non-stop, but the thoughtful dialogue throughout the tale keeps you mentally engaged on every page."

DOUGLAS E. LEE, Brigadier General, USA (Ret), President, Chaplain Alliance for Religious Liberty

ADULT HISTORICAL FICTION

"*Luther in Love*, a fitting tribute to one of the most fascinating power-couples of the ages! With the skill of a scholar and the sparkle of a bard, Douglas Bond weaves together a thrilling and engaging story."

ERIC LANDRY, Executive Editor, *Modern Reformation*

"If you enjoy reading the fictional works of C. S. Lewis, you will love *The Betrayal*."

BURK PARSONS, editor, *Tabletalk*

"In *The Thunder*, Douglas Bond deftly escorts us into the 16th century world of John Knox. Bond's careful use of language…the seamless flow, rich, vivid picture of Scotland and Reformation. The spiritual aspect of the story richer... A fine work."

LIZ CURTIS HIGGS, best-selling author of the Lowlands of Scotland series

"In *The Revolt*, Douglas Bond uses his unique writing style to produce a highly readable imagining of the travails of John Wycliffe, ...a vivid and exciting narrative..."

BOB CRESON, President/CEO, Wycliffe Bible Translators, USA

Neil Perkins, a student at Haltwhistle Grammar School in England, unearths an ancient Roman manuscript. After dedicating himself to studying Latin, he uncovers a story of treachery and betrayal from the 3rd century.

"Enjoyable reading for anyone who likes a gripping, fast-paced adventure story, *Hostage Lands* will especially delight young students of Latin and Roman history."

STARR MEADE, author of *Grandpa's Box*

Half-Saxon, half-Dane, misfit Cynwulf lives apart from the world in a salvaged Viking ship, dreaming of spending his life with the fair Haeddi. When he is accused of murder, he must clear his name before he loses everything to the vengeance of the community that has already rejected him.

"In *Hand of Vengeance* Douglas Bond shines a light on the past in a way that's as entertaining as it is informative."

JANIE B. CHEANEY, senior writer, WORLD magazine

CROWN & COVENANT TRILOGY

The Crown & Covenant trilogy follows the lives of the M'Kethe family as they endure persecution in 17ᵗʰ century Scotland and later flee to colonial America. Douglas Bond weaves together fictional characters and historical figures from Scottish Covenanting history.

"Will lift you into the 17ᵗʰ century and onto the moorlands of Scotland. This is the danger-zone, inhabited by evil, death, courage, and faith. A story not to be missed."
SINCLAIR FERGUSON, Chancellor's Professor of Systematic Theology at RTS

"Douglas Bond has introduced a new generation to the heroics of the Scottish Covenanters, and he has done it in a delightful way."
LIGON DUNCAN, Chancellor/CEO of Reformed Theological Seminary and the John E. Richards Professor of Systematic and Historical Theology